Sass, Smarts,
and
Stilettos

How Italian women make the ordinary, extraordinary.

Dear Marianne
Wishing extraordinary
you a lifetime of
extraordinary moments

Love,
Gabriella

Gabriella Contestabile

Published by Sumisura Publications Oct, 2017
ISBN: 9780996058520

Editor: Catherine Michele Adams and Fernanda Pinzon
Typeset: Greg Salisbury
Book Cover Design: Katerina Miras
Portrait Photographer: Catherine Michele Adams

DISCLAIMER: This book is a guide intended to offer information on style. Readers of this publication agree that neither the author nor her publisher will be held responsible or liable for damages that may be alleged or resulting directly or indirectly from the reading of this publication

This book is dedicated to my mother,
Clelia, of the mani d'oro (golden hands)

"Nothing arouses speculation more than the sight of a woman enjoying herself."
Luisa May Alcott

TESTIMONIALS

"An Italian lifestyle is understated, not loud, it doesn't need to brag, because it's an inherited patrimony, made of the simple things, yet luxurious and sophisticated, a tribute to quality. Gabriella does an exquisite and ambitious job at describing it in passionate detail, and in a book you won't want to put down."
Francesca Belluomini, author of 'The Cheat Sheet of Italian Style'

"I was captivated by this inspirational, heartwarming and fascinating account of what it means to be not only an Italian American woman, but a WOMAN. Framed against the backdrop of Italian life and culture, each personally-reflective chapter is filled with lessons for a rich life through history, art, fashion, architecture, philosophy, and cuisine. Humor and wit are sprinkled throughout this compelling literary work. Gabriella takes the reader on a journey that touches the heart, the mind, the senses, and ultimately, the soul. A must read and reread for every 'extraordinary' woman!"
Dr. Marie-Elena Liotta, Chairperson and Trustee of the Enrico Fermi Scholarship Foundation

"Gabriella's writing, as always, celebrates all the senses, and there you are, sitting on a mint-green Vespa wearing fashionable heels (suddenly, you won't trip in them) and the perfect perfume. Simply a must read, not just for the delicious style and lusciously painted scenes, but because this is pure inspiration of the go-get-'em variety, the kind that inspires us to reach out to the women in our lives and say, 'Do you need a helping hand? That is a fabulous scarf. Let's do this.' "

Flavia Brunetti, author of 'Young in Rome'
city blog

"Sass, Smarts and Stilettos captivates with its brilliant depiction of the Italian woman, her unapologetic way of being, her love of life and her inimitable sense of style that's deeply rooted in her cultural heritage. At its core, it is a profoundly inspiring story of humanity, art, intuition and female empowerment."

Aleksandra Lacka, Personal Brand Strategist
and Founder of insights-studio.com

TABLE OF CONTENTS

Testimonials VII

Forword...1
Introduction 5
Five Thousand Years of Gorgeousness 7

Chapter One: A Question of Education 11
Chapter Two: The Extraordinary in the Ordinary....................14
Chapter Three: From the Ashes of War 19
Chapter Four: The Legend of Italy.....................................25
Chapter Five: The Legacy of Community................................29
Chapter Six: Always Stop for Wonder.................................32
Chapter Seven: Heart, Mystery, and Mastery.........................36
Chapter Eight: The Divas of Italian Film.............................42
Chapter Nine: Food, the Talisman of Happiness......................51
Chapter Ten: Food Identity...59
Chapter Eleven: Joy in Simple Things.................................63
Chapter Twelve: A Happy Traveler in my Home Country...............72
Chapter Thirteen: Exquisitely Unconventional.......................77
Chapter Fourteen: Pieces of Homeland 83
Chapter Fifteen: Turning Sauce into Sass.............................88
Chapter Sixteen: Interconnected Fashion..............................92
Chapter Seventeen: An Extraordinary Life Involves Risk............98
Chapter Eighteen: Style is Ageless....................................102
Chapter Nineteen: Roman Holiday......................................108
Chapter Twenty: Luisa Spagnoli, Trailblazer..........................113
Chapter Twenty-One: Brunello Cucinelli, a Humanistic Enterprise 118
Chapter Twenty-Two: Alberta Ferretti, Rooted Inspiration 121
Chapter Twenty-Three: How to Live and Work Like an Italian 125
Chapter Twenty-Four: Your Life is Your Biggest Work of Art 130

Chapter Twenty-Five: Italian Women Celebrate Femininity................135
Chapter Twenty-Six: Effortless Chic 139
Chapter Twenty-Seven: She Who Spends More, Spends Less............146
Chapter Twenty-Eight: Competition Among Women is Overrated.....158
Chapter Twenty-Nine: Secrets of an Italian Woman's Skin 164
Chapter Thirty: Collaborative Love...169
Chapter Thirty-One: Tears 174
Chapter Thirty-Two: Timeless Raiment or Sustainable Chic.............177

Epilogue 183
Author Biography..185
Sass, Smarts, Stilettos, and the Su Misura (Made-to-Measure) Life.....186
Acknowledgments 189
Bibliography 190
Italian Glossary 193

FOREWORD

We are all interconnected. We are connected to people, places, emotions, experiences, and to those fleeting moments in time that may not even stay in our conscious memory, but are forever inscribed in our hearts.

Do you ever wonder why a sonata, a sculpture, a twilight bike ride, can make you feel so delighted and 'in the moment'?

I never put much thought into it, until I had the honor to write this foreword. Gabriella's book is a masterful deconstruction of 'the moment', and a holistic look at a compilation of such moments over one's lifetime; moments that merge to shape human experience, and ultimately, as the author describes it, to form a tapestry of our society. And if our society is a tapestry, Gabriella is the one who rolls out the golden thread to help us navigate, experience, and understand the richness of the world around us.

From the very first pages, we are taken on an animated journey of discovery, inspiration, and eventually, deep human connection.

While reading, I was immediately brought back to the time when I, too, walked the cobblestone streets of Rome and Florence. I could recall the aroma of fresh espresso, the grandeur of the Duomo, and the majestic Renaissance buildings with their intricate facades. I didn't even realize how much I missed being in Italy. I was amazed by how vividly I was able to recall the sensation of being there. The feeling was so familiar, although I had not experienced it in many years. Italy now feels closer than ever.

It was in Italy over a decade ago, where as a student at Cornell, I had the extraordinary opportunity to meet the late Vittorio Missoni, and learn the brand's story; the strong ethics it adhered to, and the true quality, sustainability, and higher values that Missoni represented. My view of the world of fashion was never the same again.

That visit to Missoni touched my heart and inspired me to later create Insights Studio. I now work with talented entrepreneurs from around the world to develop their own high-quality and highly-ethical brands. Brands that represent what I call, mindful luxury; authentic, quality experiences supported by strong values. To my delight, I was not the only one who was so passionate about promoting this way of living.

When I first met Gabriella through a mutual colleague, Francesca Belluomini, we immediately bonded over a meal at a charming Italian restaurant in NYC. We spent the afternoon talking about Italy, our memories growing up in another country, fashion, food, entrepreneurship, politics, and occasionally sprinkling an Italian word into the conversation. The entire experience felt so Italian that for a moment, I forgot we were in NYC. Our age or country of origin didn't matter. Our common experience and shared values brought us together. It is a bond that I believe really began years before we even met. I am convinced that we were destined to meet.

Perhaps golden threads need to cross other paths and weave together to form a distinct, visible pattern on the tapestry?

It was that meeting, and our deep conversation, which inspired me to create my first Mindful Luxury Salon - an event that brings together women entrepreneurs, authors, and thought leaders to share their work and form new collaborations.

As a speaker at the salon, Gabriella asked us to close our eyes and imagine being in our happy place and feeling all the sensations of that place. It made me think: how often do we allow ourselves to pause and notice the intangible?

Mindful experiences, masterful work, attention to detail and quality, have never been more important. They may have been forgotten in our contemporary fast-paced world of disposable materialism, but they are not lost. There is profound meaning and relevance in Gabriella's message. Our fast fashion, processed foods, and overstuffed closets are produced at great cost to people and the environment. But in the end, it's not about the material things we accumulate, what matters is how we live and experience the life around us.

Ultimately, Gabriella shows us how Italian women turn ordinary experiences into extraordinary moments. No matter what culture, demographic or ethnic heritage one comes from, she makes the extraordinary reachable. As we immerse ourselves in the pages of this book, we are able to revive those treasured memories encoded in our subconscious.

If we can create and experience those extraordinary moments, we are also capable of doing extraordinary things. Just follow Gabriella's golden thread and see where it leads you. In the author's own words: "When the magic is there, grab it."

Aleksandra Lacka
Founder of Insights Studio and Insights Atelier

INTRODUCTION

"Italian women don't quit,"
says my friend Elizabeth.

She's just returned from holidays in Lake Como, where she watched Italian women of all ages sunbathing in bikinis along the lake, zipping to work in Milano on mint green Vespas while wearing short skirts and heels, and strolling with their children through the villages of Lombardy in pretty casual wear.

Lizzie's manicured toes sit inside a pair of silvery sandals with a sexy heel. In lieu of her usual khakis and t-shirt, she wears a white piqué sundress with a touch of décolleté and a brilliant orange lipstick. I've never seen her wear lipstick. Nor have I ever seen her wear anything remotely feminine. She looks fabulous, transformed, as women always do when they return from Italy.

We're chilling over an Aperol Spritz at an Italian wine bar on the Upper West Side, not at the opera, ballet, or theater. This is not a special occasion of any sort, other than it is two days before her sixtieth birthday. She's happily married with a daughter in college — not looking to pick up the thirty-year-old Ralph Lauren model texting at the next table.

When she exclaims in wonder to me, "Italian women don't quit," she's referring of course to the Italian woman's enduring penchant for style, whatever her age, size, or socioeconomic status. Style is simply one of the most joyful portions embedded in the Italian woman's DNA.

She embraces the full power of the feminine, celebrates its liberties, laughs off its limitations, learns from its contradictions, and refuses to give these up or to give into the societal guilt that keeps other women from embracing a vital part of themselves.

I'm older than Elizabeth, but even today if I walk into Tusseda — a lingerie and swimwear shop on Via Frattina in Rome — I will be shown a bikini, maybe in warm coral, and a sarong. If I look for sandals in a shoe store in Bergamo, the sales woman will bring out a pair from the latest collection. In an artisanal dress shop off an obscure side street in Avezzano, the owner will surprise me with a dress so original and flattering, I can't resist.

On no occasion will I be shown something frumpy or dated. Whatever they show me will be an item of contemporary beauty and style. It will be of a beautiful fabric. It will fit well and have an edge of tasteful provocation. It will be an item that has fun with life.

In Italy, when a woman passes over the threshold of youth, she does not become invisible. If her body is less than perfect, she does not resign herself to years of uninspired dressing. On the contrary, she becomes even more of a master of her own physical self through what she chooses to be and what she chooses to wear. And only she knows what's best.

As a feminist who grew up with the writings of Simone de Beauvoir and of the stylish Gloria Steinem, I see no contradiction in this love of dress-up. My Diane Keaton style suits and hats share a rack with Victorian blouses and lace sundresses. My coral lipsticks and jasmine perfumes blissfully share a shelf with my dog-eared copy of *The Second Sex* and my mother's oldest cookbook, *Il Talismano della Felicità*.

But after that conversation with Elizabeth, I began to ponder the question: What is it that gives Italian women that sass, that spark to go right on with it? She's right. We don't give up. We don't say at some point in our lives, "It's too late, we're too old, we're not perfect, it's too much to hope for." We don't accept the ordinary. We dig in and do what we've always done. We get creative, and we transform it.

FIVE THOUSAND YEARS OF GORGEOUSNESS

"A sensibility that is at once opulent and relaxed. It's that joy in beauty in any setting that is very Italian."
Julie Ann Morrison, Managing Director,
Bulgari UK and Australia

If I could relive that morning I would: the damp cobbled streets of Oltrarno; the artisans rolling up gates outside their shops. A young woman on a motorino rounded the corner of Via dei Serragli. Art students balanced portfolios on handlebars and cycled past.

Marina, my morning barista, slid a perfect espresso across the counter. The first caffè at the local "bar" when one is back in Florence is just that. Perfection. Moments later, I walked along Via Santo Spirito, planning my day: visits to my favorite artisans, the Masaccio frescoes in the Brancacci Chapel, lunch with a friend at the Caffè degli Artisti, and a quick stop at the Basilica di Santo Spirito to see, for the hundredth time, one of Michelangelo's first sculptures, a small wooden crucifix, simple and magnificent.

I picked up my pace in anticipation...tap, tap. Angela Caputi rapped on the window of her jewelry atelier and waved me in. I love her look: silver hair combed back, square glasses, a gorgeously braided coral and black resin necklace made from local materials, her happy eyes.

She strung beads as we spoke. Under displays of jewelry inspired by American cinema and Tuscan history, I opened up three wide drawers layer by layer, one filled with earrings, another with bracelets, still another revealed necklaces of different lengths. I felt like a child playing dress-up or like Alice rendered small in front of a giant version of her mother's jewelry box. For this reason Angela has named her brand Giuggiù, her childhood nickname, meaning delightful little thing.

Her studio buzzed with energy and songs by Amy Winehouse. We talked and laughed over espresso. When you're in Italy the first caffè you have alone, the second is always with someone. After Angela wrapped up my purchases, we walked together to Gianni Raffaelli's engraving workshop, where I bought a print of a blue Vespa. It's my dream to move to Rome and ride through the streets of Monti on a blue Vespa, wearing high heels of course.

I watched Raffaelli apply watercolor with a fine brush to a print of the Ponte Vecchio, which he'd etched on a copper plate, inked, covered with paper, and run through a copperplate press. On an easel stood a quirkier print of Mary Poppins flying over the rooftops of London and the cupola of St. Paul's Cathedral.

To enter the understated ateliers of Florence's printmakers, mosaicists, jewelry designers, silversmiths, leather craftspeople, chocolatiers, and fabric weavers is to witness firsthand the serene but heartfelt dedication to one's craft and why these "lost arts" are not only timeless, but seriously cool.

Later that evening, under a frescoed ceiling in the glorious fifteenth-century Palazzo della Gherardesca — once home to Florentine nobles, now the Four Seasons Firenze — the city's artisans gathered together with Prosecco flutes in hand. The joy in the room was electric. You could see it in their eyes and in the warmth with which they greeted their colleagues. I imagine this is how it must feel to work every day with one's heart and hands creating objects of enduring beauty. It's like falling in love, a state in which you feel very much alive.

As a spectator that evening, I fell in love multiple times with the arts on display. Weavers from the Antico Setificio Fiorentino, Florence's oldest silk mill, had draped silks and taffetas over an armoire. The Setificio's taffeta undulated with light, rustled when you touched it, and when bunched on a table, stood up on its own.

Two models buttoned the jackets of their navy and black Stefano Ricci tuxedos and offered guests sachets made from the shantung silk of the Setificio and filled with the Officina Profumo Farmaceutica di Santa Maria Novella's signature potpourri.

Along a hallway whose enormous windows overlooked the garden, young artisans from La Scuola del Cuoio threaded strips of leather into satchels, a style reminiscent of the iconic Bottega Veneta intrecciato weave. Inside a leather box stood tools of the shoemaker's trade: the thick bristled shoe brush and a round tin of polish, reminding us that once we owned a leather item of such prized quality, we were to take care of it.

Angela Caputi clinked glasses with master perfumer Dr. Vranjes. I never leave Florence without one of his fragrances diffusers. They transport me back to Italy when I return home. He passed me a scent strip of *Aria*, a composition of orange flower, white musk, wild mint — scents redolent of the Tuscan countryside.

Mosaicists Bruno and Iacopo Lastrucci used fifteenth-century instruments to slice luminous colored stones, which they then fitted together like a jigsaw puzzle into a mosaic that, even up close, looked like an oil painting or a watercolor of Brunelleschi's Duomo.

An aroma of dark chocolate meant the ever-inventive chocolatiers of the Cioccolateria Molto Bene were close by. Alongside a palette of chocolates in irreverent shapes stood a life-sized mold of a chocolate shirt and tie.

This blend of the old and the new, spiked with a single disruptive element, is quintessentially Florentine — the very essence of what many associate with Italian design.

As we crossed the gardens and entered the Palazzo Capponi via a grand staircase into another opulent setting, so different from the humble workshops I'd visited earlier, I sensed something more, a lack of pretense. No one was in competition with anyone else. Each artisan's achievement contributed to the whole — a community of which they were all a part. This inherent grace and ethos is why Italians do everything with seemingly effortless style.

So I pondered the question: What is it like to live and work fully within one's philosophy of living, a way of life that is at once humanitarian, collaborative, and infused with a perpetual appreciation for beauty in all its forms?

It must feel exhilarating. On a certain level I can relate. It's the sensation I have the minute my feet touch ground at Fiumincino. I am at once exuberant and alive. I savor every moment, every experience. I see possibilities in the unexpected.

According to Domenico Dolce and Stefano Gabbana, a single word defines why Italian style is revered around the world: passion. It is just that passion that has yielded, in the words of British milliner Stephen Jones, "an extraordinary history of five thousand years of gorgeousness."

"Style is a simple way of saying complicated things," wrote Jean Cocteau. Italian artisanship and style in matters traditional and avant-garde, draw upon heritage, community, sensory acuity gleaned through centuries of living in the most sensual country on earth, and a profound love of the arts.

This immersion yields a life fully lived. Love of beauty, respect for humankind and our planet are qualities embedded in every Italian, and in Italian women in particular. As they will tell you, "It's a question of educazione."

ONE

A Question of Education

"Elegance is a Question of Education"
Sacha Guitry

y mother Clelia unspooled the fabric from its cardboard rectangle. Three rolls, three thumps, and it spilled over the table in luminous waves. I wanted to touch it, but her look, I knew it well, stopped me. Dusty rose crêpe de chine, light as air, now freed up for her capable hands to fold into a triangle and place across my chest.

I knew not to move because she was, in that moment, considering the form this dress would take: long and flowing, or short and tailored? Will it be a single straight line, or do we cut at the waist and attach a gathered or a bias-cut skirt? We could stitch two parallel seams down the front, one on either side starting mid-shoulder, but then we will need to cut the fabric into three sections and sew in a lining.

My mother explained that since this was a lot of fabric, we should do a long sleeve with a deep cuff and covered buttons. She gathered it up into puckered folds to show me how it would drape. My silver shoes with the ankle strap would look perfect with it, the ones we bought from the artigiano in Burano, she reminded me. So not only did I feel myself firmly planted on that color-drenched island in Venice, I had also entered the alta moda world of my mother's imagination. I was seventeen and I'd already figured out the details: frosted pink lipstick, bone-straight hair, glittery handbag with the chain handle she'd found for me at Bergdorf's.

It was the '60s, the era of silver stockings à la Twiggy. She'd trained me over the years to make those associations; to think about the one accessory, a color, or a particular way to roll the cuff of a shirt or to flip up a collar, giving an outfit that *je ne sais quoi* that says Italian.

This was why we flipped through the pages of *Vogue*, which I'd brought with me. It was one of those mother-daughter afternoons when we didn't argue. We'd stepped into a harmonious space where it was all about the fabric and the dress. One we loved to inhabit together. It was like walking into a concert hall and giving yourself up to the music. All that mattered was the now.

It was the now that my mother seized upon to talk about style and the *educazione* it required. For her educazione had multiple meanings. There was the academic kind. And then there was the other kind, the educazione that dictated how one received guests, what one ate, how one dressed, and the respect we conferred on our environment and fellow humans.

On that day educazione told her she would make small covered buttons for the sleeves in this dress. They were the most pragmatic and aesthetic choice. Otherwise she would choose the mother of pearl ones inside a glass display case, which were perhaps too expensive. Details made the dress. Cheap buttons would ruin the entire effect, especially when the fabric was this exquisite.

It was the same with accessories. Good (always Italian) shoes will make an ordinary dress look extraordinary, she said. And the opposite, shoes of poor quality, make even the most elegant designer gown ordinary. I learned early on that, as far as my mother was concerned, ordinary was even worse than awful.

The word educazione came up often in our household. Someone

who was courteous, knowledgeable, and well dressed was considered *educata* or *educato*. It was a person who didn't rush to judge others.

In contrast a rude or unkind person was simply maleducata. A donna educata knew to dress well when invited to an event or to someone's home. It was not a question of labels or monies spent, but a sign of respect for the host and the occasion. It implied a level of care and attention. It was about *la bella figura* — the indelible first impression, a rule that applied in every setting, whether it be a gala inside the Pierre Hotel or a backyard barbecue.

The confluence of the word educazione with style and dress, and with the uncanny ability to transform even the most mundane of tasks into an extraordinary experience, has captured my attention all these years. Especially since I see the same pervasive thinking in my Italian and Italian-American women friends, regardless of where they were born, how many generations removed, or wherever they live in the world. So I had to delve into it, and my mother's history seemed like a good place to start.

TWO

THE EXTRAORDINARY IN THE ORDINARY

"The hours that ordinary people waste, extraordinary people leverage."
Robin Sharma

Transforming the ordinary into extraordinary comes naturally to Italians. Two world wars, suffering, and scarcity drove a populace to seek beauty and joy in what little one had. It inspired a national pride in Italy's stunning natural landscapes, artisan traditions, and unrivaled artistic richness. It forced a certain frugality. One bought less and bought better; the few quality items one needed had to be beautiful and durable. This principle morphed into a way of life. *L'arte d'arrangiarsi* — the art of figuring out a way to do what one needed to do, in order to make not only a living but also a life worth living — became an Italian mantra.

Consider the simplicity of rubbing a piece of crusty bread in olive oil; a fresh green salad with lemon and oil; my mother's broth flavored by celery, onions, carrots, some tomato, and nothing else; a drizzle of honey over chunks of pecorino; a *granita al caffè* in a piazza. Solutions and inventions had to marry beauty with pragmatism. A criteria which survives to this day, and which is responsible, in no small part, for Italy's prolific achievements in art, architecture, science, culinary arts, and the entire spectrum of design. It's what gives the coveted label Made In Italy both its sexiness and its currency.

Within this framework it's not surprising that young women of my mother's generation would seek artisanal outlets both for pleasure and practicality. They learned to knit and sew so to make their own clothing. Clelia took it a few steps further. First, she trained with the local *sarta* so she could one day make the glamorous gowns she saw in movies. Even then, she saw no limit to her own future mastery of the craft. She studied the lace dress with the mandarin collar and swirling skirt that Vera-Ellen wore as she tapped and twirled with Danny Kaye in *White Christmas*. She would remake it; indeed, she would inhabit it, her way — an Italian way.

She knew well those other unforgettable lace dresses, like the one worn by Audrey Hepburn as Princess Anne in the final scene of *Roman Holiday*, in which a reporter asks which part of her European tour is most memorable. She hesitates, looks at Gregory Peck, with whom she's fallen in love. She raises her head, elegantly capped with a smart hat, and says with conviction, "Rome. By all means Rome."

Roma è solo una, my mother would say. There is only one Rome.

However, Clelia's most dominant heroines weren't the actresses of Hollywood but the defiant divas of Italian film. And while Gina, Sophia, Giulietta, Claudia, and the inimitable earth goddess Anna Magnani were part of a rarified world she would never be a part of, the circumstances of her life did not prevent Clelia from learning to create what she could never afford to buy. And she would do one thing more. Not only did she master the knitting machine, she even went so far as to establish a thriving business of her own. No other woman in Antrosano had ever done such a thing.

Audaciously, this most brazen of Francesco and Laura's seven daughters had devised a larger plan. She would knit original, fashion-forward sweaters, dresses, and baby blankets for the local townspeople. She would break the rules and they'd like it. They would pay her, which they eventually did without questioning her high prices. And one day she'd make enough money to realize her ultimate dream: to study nursing at the Ospedale del Bambin Gesù, a hospital on Janiculum Hill in Rome, the most seductive city on earth.

At the same time, in their mother's atelier near Parma, three sisters were also striking out in the fashion world, working hard to perfect their craft: Micol, Giovanna, and Zoe Fontana, who'd learned to sew and tailor as soon as they were old enough to hold a needle and scissors. When they grew up, they went their separate ways to apprentice at different ateliers and couture houses in Paris and Milan. It was Zoe who, upon returning to Italy, took the first train out of Milan, determined to go wherever it led. It was destined for Rome.

In the years following World War I, France, with Paris as its Mecca, dominated every aspect of haute couture. But this did not deter the three sisters who, in 1943, in the midst of World War II, opened their own workshop, Sorelle Fontana, in Palazzo Orsini in Rome. They introduced the world to the coveted signature Fontana style. This house DNA, born of tireless cultivation and passion, yielded exquisitely tailored and delicately embellished dresses in sumptuous fabrics. With each passing year came more innovations from the House of Fontana, where they pioneered the use of printed cloth and gave Italian fashion a look and a life of its own.

It was that spark that drew a young Clelia and her girlfriends to their atelier. One morning, while strolling past the store, Clelia spotted a pair of black suede evening pumps in the window. They were unusual, with a higher front, bisected by pleated satin accents like the cummerbund of a man's tuxedo.

Since she didn't own a tuxedo, and it would be many years before YSL introduced his venerable *smoking* for women, she bought the shoes and hired a *sarta* to make her an ottoman coat. It is still today a work of art, nipped at the waist with a princess-like flare that opens up with pleats in the back, lapels embroidered with velvet flowers and tiny pearls. I can see it resurrected today in a collection by Miu Miu or Dolce and Gabbana and even worn with a pair of vintage jeans. Timeless good taste, imagination, garments that multi-task, and garments that re-invent themselves decade after decade: These are four defining qualities of Italian sartorial design. Women of my mother's post-war generation saw and participated in both its birth and evolution.

Clelia must have sensed this as she wandered the streets of the city like a child at Luna Park. This was where Italy's fashion currency came to life, where the movers and shakers dug in their heels and said, "We're here." Fernanda Gattinoni was already designing draped evening and tailored daywear for Eva Peron and the Maharani of Palampur. Elsa Schiaparelli, whose disdain for conformity led her to collaborations with Man Ray and Dalí, upended conventional paradigms of beauty and pioneered the concept of ugly chic. The flame had been lit like an Olympic torch, and The Games were set to begin. While Avezzano and other small towns throughout Italy had their tailors and dressmakers, Rome was home to the aristocratic and adventurous dressmakers of the wealthy.

Young women born into noble families channeled their aesthetic expression through fabrics and styling, among them the Marchesa Olga di Grésy, Princess Irene Galitzine, Simonetta Colonna di Cesarò, and the Countess Gabriella di Robilant, founder of Gabriellasport and a member of the international jet set that included Cole Porter, Elsa Maxwell, and Jean Patou. Jean Patou credited the *assoluta* (grand diva) of Italian style, Elsa Schiaparelli, for her decision to enter the world of fashion. Years later, a journalist in *Grazia* would praise these "brave young women" for using their ingenuity and aesthetic brilliance to "pull the elegance out of the ruins of Italy."

Hollywood took notice. As American filmmakers flocked to Rome's *Cinecittà* in search of lower production costs and a warm climate, Italian fashion started to gain traction. Then one morning, Gioia Marconi, daughter of the scientist and inventor Guglielmo Marconi, paid a visit to the Fontana sisters and introduced them to Linda Christian.

THREE

FROM THE ASHES OF WAR

"The craftsmanship is incredible. Whether you are rich or you are poor growing up in Italy you have an appreciation for beauty."
Tom Ford, designer and filmmaker

"Italian fashion is different for two reasons; it's sleeker and it's sexier. You would never mistake an Italian cut dress from a French one."
Nicholas Coleridge, Condé Nast

On a sunny winter morning in 1949, Linda Christian and Tyrone Power were married at the church of Santa Francesca Romana in Rome, only steps from the Colosseum. The medieval church was filled with so many white flowers, it was almost impossible to see the stunning Mexican-American actress walk through its massive doors. The groom wore a Caraceni morning suit. But it was Linda's dress that took everyone's breath away. Designed and hand sewn by the still relatively new Fontana sisters, using fifty yards of satin, seventy yards of lace, and two thousand pearls, the gown's shimmering train fanned out and trailed behind the couple almost the entire length of the steps below.

It was one of those dreamlike Hollywood on the Tiber moments, etched into cinema and fashion history. The Power–Christian wedding was the most talked about event of that era. Fontana's dress made international newsreels and headlines. Fashion magazines described its construction in minute detail. The gorgeousness of its fabric was lauded in world capitals. This dress marked the pivotal moment when Italy's fledgling fashion industry took flight. Its reputation has soared ever since.

This apotheosis of gorgeousness has its genesis in the innate Italian penchant for creating beauty, even from the ashes of war. As Italy freed itself from fascism and Parisian dominance, Italian fashion had to stake out its own cultural terrain and find its own voice. There was no autonomous self-referential fashion language, no established school of design. It had to tell its own story, so it drew from the external resources all around: its landscape, its artisan traditions, and the cultural frameworks in which Italy took great pride — art and architecture.

It was a fortuitous choice. In Italy, then as now, tradition and modernity, the old and the new in fashion, architecture, home, and industrial design, all blend together as effortlessly as the drape of a Pucci gown.

In the earliest part of the twentieth century, dressmaker and activist Rosa Genoni, inspired by the artists of the *quattrocento*, drew from Botticelli's painting *La Primavera* to give a renaissance patina to her embroidered evening dresses. Years later, Pucci prints would reproduce the glass mosaics of the cloisters in Monreale, Sicily, and the colors of the Palio di Siena. Armani would channel the architectural and industrial design ethic of Milan to design suits of impeccable fit and styling. And a trail-blazing young Miuccia Prada inherited a prominent leather goods company, only to turn tradition on its head and launch a nylon backpack whose iconic logo would challenge every tenet of fashion from that day forward.

After the war, Italy's strong relationship with the United States as ally and trading partner did much to propel these nativist talents forward and to install the defining parameters of Italian designer Ready To Wear: beautiful textiles, fine tailoring, and artisanal leather production. A welcome infusion of aid through the Marshall Plan, specifically targeted to the fashion industry and its related textile businesses, planted the seed for a thriving fashion industry and the emergence of the Italian "economic miracle."

In 1950, as Italy continued to emerge from the devastation of the war, the Brooklyn Museum hosted an exhibit entitled "Italy at Work." Its organizers had decided it was time to show American retailers and distributors of all Italy was capable. It presented the very best of Italian craftsmanship in textiles, leatherwork, ceramics, and glass.

One year later, and only two years after Linda Christian had introduced the world to the Fontana sisters, Giovanni Battista Giorgini, a prophetic entrepreneur and marketer from Lucca, sent out the following request — nested within an invitation to Italy's very first fashion show, La Sala Bianca, in his home at 144 Via dei Seragli in Florence:

The aim of the evening is to give emphasis to our fashion. Ladies are keenly invited to wear clothes of purely Italian inspiration.

Although post-war Paris had re-aligned itself with traditional French haute couture, Giorgini knew that Italy's fiery new ready-to-wear designers were ready to strut their entrepreneurial verve on the world stage. The Power–Christian wedding had lit the flame. Heritage and tenacity would do the rest.

Giorgini worked his connections with the *cognoscenti* in the international marketplace. Emboldened by the overwhelming success of Italian exports, due in no small part to the Brooklyn Museum exhibit, he invited American retailers and entrepreneurs to the Sala Bianca to view the transformative collections of Countess Simonetta Visconti, the young sculptor Roberto Capucci, the Sorelle Fontana (the Fontana sisters), Emilio Schuberth, Jole Veneziani, and a brash Florentine-born Caprese named Emilio Pucci.

As the designers sent their creations down the runway before American buyers and journalists, the world took note of the quality, aesthetic, and dynamism that would establish and define Italian Ready To Wear for decades to come.

From then on, American, Italian and other European actresses flocked to the Sorelle Fontana for romantic and elegant dresses fashioned in the new Italian Style. The sisters were the era's Vera Wang; their wedding dresses, the most cited and most coveted in the world. Audrey Hepburn commissioned a dress for her marriage to James Hanson, though she cancelled the wedding while filming *Roman Holiday*, asking that the sisters give the dress away. "I want my dress to be worn by another girl for her wedding, perhaps someone who couldn't ever afford a dress like mine, the most beautiful, poor Italian girl you can find." She finally gave it to a young woman from the town of Latina named Amabile Altobella.

While they sought to Italianize everything French, the Fontana look still borrowed extensively from the Dior collection of 1947. This one event, Christian Dior's very first collection, established him, rightfully, as one of the most important couturiers of the twentieth century. His timing was perfect. A ruinous world war had ended. People had grown tired of sartorial restrictions and shortages, and the prevalent military and civilian uniformity in fashion.

Women were ready to respond, not only to a new look, but also to a new outlook. On that gray and very cold day of February 12, with coal rationed and in short supply, Dior, an unknown designer, unveiled his new collection and new silhouette in a private mansion on Avenue Montaigne. While few journalists attended, those who did, proclaimed the birth of a fashion revolution.

The look was fresh: rounded shoulders, full and fitted bodices, hand-span waists over voluminous swirling skirts in gorgeous fabrics, colors, and prints. Fashion became joyful and expressive, and Dior was taken aback by his own success. "I had the charming surprise of discovering that even young women fell in love with the new fashion. It was the style of youth and the future." Dior had named his first collection Corolle (Petal), but the journalist Carmel Snow anointed it with the name the fashion world would never forget — the New Look.

The Fontana sisters took that vision further, creating glamorous and consistently flattering dresses in fantastical designs and prints. The female form had been celebrated in Italian painting and in sculpture for centuries, and what a better place to seek out inspiration than in Rome. I don't know if the Fontana Sisters at the time had been as awestruck as I was by Antonio Canova's sensuous *Pauline Bonaparte*, by Bernini's luminous *Daphne in Metamorphoses*, or by his magnificent female figure of *Truth* inside the Galleria Borghese, a piece considered the quintessential baroque sculpture and his most personal work. Did they study the young beautiful face of Mary in Michelangelo's *Pietà* or the colors and draping of fabrics in the paintings of the young Raffaello?

One cannot live in a city such as Rome or Florence without falling in love with art — or without developing that second sense that makes one stop, no matter how frenzied the day, to find beauty in even the simplest object or occurrence. The organic outgrowth of that quest is an implacable desire to replicate beauty in the form of art, perhaps not the art of the masters, but art in all its organic and evolutionary forms, including fashion, design, and the culinary arts, from whatever part of the world did it best.

Barring that possibility, because perhaps one cannot become, for whatever reason, a designer or a chef, then one looks to make art of the ordinary, even the mundane. The entire spectrum of daily life is fair game, accessible to all our pleasure-seeking senses. Therefore, in Italy, life transforms itself into the ultimate art form. How could it be otherwise?

Consider that a brazen young woman, one of seven sisters, born to a vineyard owner and his wife, in a small mountain village with no telephone or running water, would replicate the Dior look in her own wedding dress one year before the Power–Christian wedding. Clelia would find a photograph in the magazine *Grazia*, tear it out and tape it to her wall so she could look at it every day for a month. Gradually, she began to edit it in her mind. With a piece of charcoal on a sketchpad, she drew her own interpretation and told her mother's *sarta*, "This is what I want. Lace over satin, a fitted waist, cut a tiny bit below the waist for a softer flow, a gentle gathering, pleating in the back to initiate a modest train. The train should fan out in wider pleats below to show the swirled flowers and leaves imprinted in the *pizzo* (lace). And we will have small covered buttons run from the nape of the neck, down the spine. Tiny buttons that closed with hand-knotted loops. Each sleeve would gather a touch at the shoulders for volume, then fall to just below the elbow, where it would button in a tight cuff all the way to the wrist."

Of course the young bride couldn't see thirty-plus years into the future when, on an auspicious August morning, I would walk into the flagship Christian Dior boutique on Avenue Montaigne in Paris, in the same space where Dior introduced his iconic collection, to buy my own white velvet wedding dress for a winter wedding. When I phoned from Paris and shared my choice, all she said was *"Brava."*

I thanked her, for both the dress and her validation. Because, while I had not inherited Clelia's *mani d'oro* (hands of gold) or her infinite patience and talents, she had given to me the gift of her aesthetic and her affinity for a brilliant young French designer who influenced so many and died much too soon.

FOUR

The Legend of Italy

"It was indeed a piece of the best of Italy, the most serious, brilliant, strong, honest, tenacious, hard-working and intelligent."
Dino Buzzati, journalist

I'm four years old in the photo. I wear a white angora coat and a bonnet-style cap, and I'm sitting on a suitcase on the deck of the *Andrea Doria*, ready to make the transatlantic crossing from the port of Genova to North America. My father had been transferred from the *Ministero degli Affari Esteri* (The Ministry of Foreign Affairs) in Rome to the Italian embassy in Ottawa, Canada.

With us came a *baule* — a giant trunk — carrying our dresses and suits, shoes in felt bags, velvet boxes of jewelry. There was a lavender-scented drawer for my father's linen handkerchiefs and my mother's embroidered ones. Another drawer held my father's shaving accessories, my mother's crystal perfume atomizers, tortoise-shell combs and hairbrushes. That drawer smelled of leather and wood — but also of the comfort of a late night by the portholes in our stateroom, when the stars lit up the endless night sky and my father read out loud from Italo Calvino's book of Italian folktales.

Given such details, you might assume we were part of a privileged class. We weren't, but my parents always believed in the adage *Compra meno, compra meglio* —- buy less, buy better. One owned a few things, but only the best, and we took care of them forever. Back then it was not uncommon for a first-generation Italian family of modest means to have clothes custom-made by a local *sarto* or *sarta* in their hometown. We never had a lavish amount of things, but enough for me to delight in when my mom unclipped the bronze latches of the *baule* and swung open the two halves to reveal the row of leather-tasseled drawers on one side, and, on the other, thick wooden hangers draped with a few fine wool suits, silk ties, satin evening dresses, my mother's embroidered shawl, and sweaters in patterns she'd copied from French fashion magazines.

The daily recurring scents of cedar, gardenia, and lavender ushered in each day's events: my father's lavender aftershave before our morning walk around the outside decks to watch the seagulls soar above the open sea; my mother's gardenia perfume, dabbed behind her ears as we stepped out of our stateroom to go to dinner. I loved the whiff of cedar whenever my father took out his navy gabardine jacket made by Enrico, the sarto we visited every time we returned to Italy. At night, after the porter brought cognac to my parents and a ceramic pot of hot chocolate for me, we'd settle in and look out the portholes at the full moon and the darkening sea.

This was officially the Andrea Doria's maiden voyage. Named after a sixteenth-century Genoese admiral and heralded as the fastest, safest, largest ship of the Italian fleet, she stood as an icon of national pride in a country trying to restore its economy and stature after World War II. *Andrea Doria* marked the beginning of a golden age for the Italian line. She was the first, to be followed by the *Cristoforo Colombo, Giulio Cesare, Michelangelo,* and *Leonardo Da Vinci.* Many today consider her to have been one of the most beautiful luxury liners ever built, on par with Cunard's majestic Queens — RMS *Queen Elizabeth* and RMS *Queen Mary* — and France's revered SS *Normandie.*

Chapter Four

The design and construction of the Andrea Doria had been a national enterprise to which Italy gave its best engineers, architects, artists, artisans and workers. She was large enough to accommodate over 1,200 passengers in three distinct and strictly segregated classes. Separate accommodations and public areas connected via corridors along the full length of the ship. I loved running up and down all of them, grabbing the polished wood handrails from side to side whenever the ship listed, which it did far too often.

For my parents and for Italians on the mainland, Andrea Doria was more than a luxury liner. She was a living testimonial to Italy's stature as a world heritage site, a mosaic at sea carrying Italy's best: its contemporary arts, splendid fabrics, iridescent enamels, and artisanal crafts. In the words of her most prominent creator, the Milanese architect Gio Ponti, and echoed by my father, Andrea Doria was to represent the "legend of Italy," a floating museum of art, technology, and timeless Italian good taste.

To underscore this meaning to the travelers on board, Ponti commissioned the Sicilian artist Salvatore Fiume to paint a full-wall mural titled *The Legend of Italy* in the first-class main lounge. In this large-scale work, Fiume integrated art and architecture into a multi-dimensional depiction of Italian spaces, its piazzas, its loggias, and its masterpieces. Before their feet ever touched upon Italian soil, travelers would know the great artistic and engineering traditions of this arresting land.

My mother liked to point out the splayed perspective in another mural, Feast of Neptune by Piero Zuffi, in which renaissance arches and stairways receded behind the bronze statue of Admiral Andrea Doria. Years later, after the *Andrea Doria* was no more, she would talk nostalgically about the ceramic panels by Guido Gambone in the Winter Garden. But her favorite work on the ship, predictably, had to do with fabric: a tapestry created by the Manifattura Italiana Tessuti e Affini of Genoa Nervi. "It's something I can touch, at least in my mind," she said, although she held me back when, while on the ship, I tried to grab it.

On the day of our approach into New York harbor, *Andrea Doria* encountered rough winter storms, causing it to list dramatically. As frightening as that experience was for all of us who travelled the final leg of that internationally publicized maiden voyage, we were greeted by great jubilation from cheering crowds and the city's Italian-American mayor, Vincent Impellitteri.

Three years later on the evening of July 26, 1956, my teary-eyed parents called me into the living room to look at the televised wreckage of the Andrea Doria, which sank after being hit by the SS Stockholm only a few miles from Nantucket. It was so many years ago, but I still remember the indescribable sense of loss. Here we were, comfortably nestled in our new Canadian home, but a vibrant part of our history had disappeared below the seas. I thought of the frescoes and the tapestries, the menus printed on parchment, decorated with colorful pen and ink drawings and calligraphy, held open by braided tassels.

On the front page of Il *Corriere della* Sera the next day, journalist Dino Buzzati wrote, "A piece of Italy is gone with the terrifying rapidity of marine disasters, and now lies buried in the deep of the ocean. It was indeed a piece of the best of Italy, the most serious, brilliant, strong, honest, tenacious, hard-working, and intelligent."

Looking back, I see what a great opportunity it was to travel on a virtual museum at sea, inside a floating testimonial to Italian heritage. But it also conveyed the realization that something so beautiful is so easily lost. This belief that joyful moments are fleeting is captured in the Italian's sense of fatalism.

Our Italian mothers have taught us that there is a point when, regardless of your best efforts, fate can take over and change course. All the more important to grab hold of those small, cherished opportunities to live fully and in real time, and to let go of anxiety. We can't control it all. In Italy, and everywhere else in the world, time is currency. Take a deep breath, and spend it well.

FIVE

THE LEGACY OF COMMUNITY

*"There is no end. There is no beginning. There is only
the infinite passion of life."*
Federico Fellini, filmmaker

While the Andrea Doria was no more, Italians who emigrated never wavered in their commitment to heritage. They looked for it in their new homeland. Where it didn't exist, they created it. And since it's in every Italian's DNA to find beauty and joy in every experience, Italians continued to re-invent themselves. They did this, wherever they lived in the world, through the building of community.

Of all the homes we lived in during my childhood, the apartment on Bank Street in Ottawa will forever be the one I miss the most. This may explain why I now live in a pre-war apartment with old world details, each room veering off from the entrance foyer. The layout implies a continuity of movement. When everyone is home, even while separately working on different projects, there's a pleasant buzz and energy I will miss one day when we are fewer.

The Ottawa apartment had high ceilings, inlaid wood floors, and huge windows that looked out over a main street. On any given day, I saw Mounties in brilliant red coats ride by on horses; dairy carts pulled by slower, geriatric equines; trams swerve along metal tracks; the entrances into three parks, one of which encircled my beloved Rideau Canal where I dreamed I would one day learn to skate like Sonja Henie.

We were on a high floor, and our building took up the entire block except for a gas station below. Since we didn't own a car, it made no sense to go there except to pump air into our bike tires on our way to the parks. Biking, walking, and tram were the best ways to get around. My school, the Italian Embassy where my father worked, and the language school where my mother took English classes were just a few tree-lined blocks away. Our bank and our local grocery were just across the street, and we weren't far from Birk's, where my mother bought silver and crystal because our dining table had to make a *bella figura* when we had guests.

Indeed so many cultural and daily places were nearby: Parliament Hill; the Experimental Farm with its brilliant tulip gardens; our local library, where the librarian would let me take out many more books than permitted; an ever-growing cadre of new Italian and Canadian friends. The proximity of everything gave us an important sense of community in a city so much larger than Avezzano.

It also provided ample opportunity for imaginative play. The best was the flat pebbled roof of an adjacent building. My friends and I would climb onto it from my bedroom window. We played hide-and-seek around the chimneys and water towers, and staged make-shift theater productions to which we sold tickets. We wrote our own scripts and performed in costumes made from our parents' discarded clothes. The opening and closing curtains consisted of two fringed bedspreads tied with ribbons on either side of a clothesline. My friend Andrew worked the gramophone inside, crawling in and out of the window to drop in new 45s and turn up the volume until neighbors complained. Being Canadian, they did so politely.

On sunny days, we took out our plastic tables, chairs and tea sets.

Chapter Five

Tea sets were commonplace in toy stores, perhaps due to Canada's still being part of the British Commonwealth. We filled the cups with lemonade and spilled pebbles on plastic plates to replicate sweets. Our mothers often brought out heartier fare in the form of sandwiches, apples, and petits fours from the French bakery. After twilight, we all climbed back through the window and said our good byes, friends running out into the hall, and up and down the stairs to respective apartments. As far as we were concerned, the entire building was our home turf — our medieval castle with its own moat, the canal two blocks away, at the end of which stood the ultimate castle. With the stately Chateau Laurier just a short adventure away, we felt justified in professing 691 Bank Street of equal stature.

Joanna's old-fashioned soda shop downstairs became our other in-house hangout. The long steel and linoleum counter had stools you could spin around on until you were dizzy. On Sunday nights, when we dealt cards and played *scopa* on the dining room table, my father would send me downstairs to buy what the Canadians called pop and the Americans called soda. My assignment: to return with a cardboard carton filled with six pop bottles in different flavors — Black Cherry, Cream, Sarsaparilla, Lemon-Lime, Orange, and Canada Dry Ginger Ale.

Drinking soda (or pop) never became a practice in our household. But the colorful sugary drinks in bottles frosted over by their immersion in ice water remained a fun part of our Sunday night ritual. It was yet another way to enter our new community with inclusiveness and on our own terms. By bringing in even a small piece of this new world into our lives, we turned an ordinary Sunday evening into something special.

SIX

STOP FOR WONDER

"Treat the earth well. It was not given to you by your parents — it was loaned to you by your children."
Native American proverb

The extraordinary can enter one's life in a flash and at whim. And that's a good thing. We become accustomed to our way of being. We craft a set of expectations. We set limits. But one day, when we slow down, open our eyes, and create the space, we see something that wakes us up.

When Queen Elizabeth II came to visit Ottawa with Prince Philip and her two children, Charles and Anne, her black motorcar passed just below our living room windows. We leaned out with our small Canadian flags in time to see her wave a gloved hand from under a fur stole. She always wore a hat, usually with a tilted brim and veil, and a dark tailored suit. While Clelia considered this the epitome of chic, I was disappointed our queen didn't dress like queens and princesses in storybooks. "She isn't wearing anything special," I said. "She looks like everyone else."

"You will have the opportunity when she returns to open Parliament," said my mother. "I read she plans to wear her tiara and her coronation gown for the occasion."

My mother's promise satisfied, especially since Parliament Hill was so close. I loved going there in winter when the gothic buildings were encrusted with snow and decorated with small colored lights. My favorite part was the Library of Parliament. Stepping into this showpiece of High Victorian Gothic Revival architecture was like stepping into one of my most beloved literary works or into a period film complete with costumes and grand ballrooms. I had never seen so many books. Under a dome in the center stood a white marble statue of a very young Queen Victoria.

That day, watching the unfolding spectacle, I decided I could gladly wait for Queen Elizabeth's future visit to Parliament. In the meantime, I kept leaning out the window to take in the rest of the parade and the noble beauty of Canada's First Nations People. I leaned out so far my mother had to grab my shoes to keep me from falling out the window.

As the sun shone down on billowing white headdresses and beaded vests in colors I had never imagined, on hair as luminous as black lacquer, I knew I was looking at some of the most beautiful people on earth. This was yet another world brought into our smaller world after an ocean crossing, set against the red, gold, and orange maple leaves of Canada's foliage, and it all seemed to fit.

From that day on, a different First Nations doll would appear on my doll shelf every three months. Each one had tawny golden skin and wore outfits of faux leather in white or tan, decorated with beads in multiple colors. Alongside these and my Eskimo dolls stood an eclectic collection of dolls from different regions of Italy: Campania, Abruzzo, Lazio, Toscana and Sicilia, each wearing her own regional costume.

When my mother and I went to the sewing notions stores, we were drawn to rolls of ribbons in sunburnt colors and geometric patterns. For years my mother used them to trim my dresses or to tie up napkins for dinner, and there was always at least one in my hair. It became another way to relive all the joyful sensations of the parade on that day.

What I remember most was our sinking into that sense of wonder born of colors, sunshine, gleaming skin, beads. There was no hurry to do something more important. We stopped to take in every color and sensation. We wove it into our lives, much like the plaiting of my braids, strands of perception woven one over the other into a pattern that said, even with our differences, we were still one vibrant and interlocking community.

That image of Canada's First Nations People had a transformative effect. While films often portrayed North American Indians as aggressors, I saw a different image, painted in my memory like the colors of the leaves on that autumn day. There was no way such regal people, riding so straight and tall on their horses, wearing magnificent headdresses and beaded leather vests made with their own hands, could commit the atrocities I saw on the screen. The chief who rode ahead of his tribe that day had eyes filled with goodness. I was sure of it. I was sure there was more than a single story to tell.

Fast forward into the twenty-first century and the opening night of the Metropolitan Museum of Art's exhibit, *The Plains Indians: Artists of the Earth and Sky*. The title alone suggested art born of a love of one's natural world, and what a world it was! What the North American Plains Indians woke up to every morning was the sweet scent of clean air, lush earth, and a stunning expanse of earth and sky; colors painted by nature's brush. And every night, they'd lie down under a sky full of stars, the hum of cicadas luring them to sleep.

They traveled along endless fertile plains in search of food and land on which to set up their homes. They saw these magnificent plains and crystal clear river waters as blessings bestowed on them. They nurtured the land that gave them sustenance, and made art of the tools and artifacts they needed to survive. As explorers and colonists from the Americas and Europe took over the vast territories and forced the Native Americans to move their homes over and over again, eventually restricting them to reservations, the Plains Community become even more resourceful and more intent on expressing its world view.

As I looked more closely at the handicrafts resembling those I'd seen from an apartment window when I was nine years old, a more complete story took hold. A Lakota horse effigy honored a horse that died in battle. Beaded symbols on a coat told of a desire to restore harmony and balance to an increasingly more dangerous world. An elaborate pipe had been shared with tradesmen and explorers. In the 1800s, life stories were etched as figures on sheets of animal hide, and in the 1900s, via easel art. Throughout the centuries, even as their world changed, the Plains Indians continued to embrace new artistic traditions and mediums to tell their stories to the world, thereby keeping their heritage alive.

So my understanding of North American First Nations People had come full circle; from a parade in Ottawa in 1958 to an exhibit in New York in 2015. That spark of wonder over fifty years ago started it all.

Never underestimate an immediate, visceral reaction — this realization reinforced within me — no matter how many years in your past. If you stopped to listen with the openness of a child, even briefly back then, it will connect with a moment in your present. It will dispel the single story and the stereotypes that deprive us of deeper truths and human connection.

If you want to make life extraordinary, enter these worlds whenever you can: try that new cuisine, travel to a place you've never been, see animals in their natural habitat, dance and sing along at the national parades, learn another language, talk to people whose lives and customs are different from your own, invite them in and create new communities. It's never too late to live a life that makes you feel fully alive.

SEVEN

HEART, MYSTERY, AND MASTERY

*"The mediator between the head and the hand has to
be the heart"*
Fritz Lang's Metropolis

L ife is a constant process of learning and unlearning. We move up two rungs of a ladder only to slip back down. But then there's the fun and the challenge of figuring out a new way to climb. It's a journey from the head to the hand. In our minds, we will ourselves to reach the top of the ladder, master the stick shift, and land the perfect tennis serve.

We see ourselves master second and third languages, trek in Bhutan, and balance our checkbook out to the penny. Sometimes the hand responds. Often it doesn't. Like a surly adolescent, it defies us. It makes mistakes. It needs an intermediary.

At least that's what I prayed for during the early Canada years. An intermediary. Because I was so young, I was not so concerned about our foreignness. Many of our family friends were Italian, as were our local shopkeepers, and the annual Christmas parties at the Embassy helped to sustain a sense of community for expatriates. My mother would take English classes at night and study from a book with drawings of stick figures doing or saying things. Overall, I felt comfortable with the pace of my language learning, and classmates never made fun of my mispronunciation or snickered when I didn't know the meaning of a word.

The only time I felt like an outsider was when I was doing what I most loved to do: reading. All the characters in my schoolbooks had short Anglo Saxon names that ended in a consonant. I so wanted a simple last name like Jones or Smith, and a cute first name like Sally. In total, there were ten syllables in my first and last name combined, and when we went around the room to introduce ourselves, my classmates were up and down in a flash, but I had to stand for what felt like forever, articulating endless vowels and consonants.

Other than that, if there were ethnic tensions, I wasn't aware of them. Switching from Italian to English became as natural as breaking an icicle off a tree branch on the way to school. My father's British accented English continued to impress, and everyone was patient when my mother spoke slowly to ensure every phrase was grammatically correct.

I found it remarkable that even though my father finished schooling only through the eighth grade, and my mother the fifth, both of my parents were eloquent speakers and writers. My father's writing style was more formal than the norm, due to his diplomatic work at the Embassy. My mother's writing was more descriptive, and I'm convinced my love of writing came from her.

It did so in an unintended way. I failed miserably in my penmanship classes. The nuns at Blessed Sacrament insisted we learn to write freehand without resting our elbows on our desks. I tried, but could never mimic the steady flowing script my parents and many of my classmates achieved with seemingly little effort. To add to my embarrassment, Sister Bernice informed the class that Western handwriting had been developed from early fourteenth-century Florentine cursive. The Italians had a knack for beautiful handwriting, she said, raising her eyebrows at the foreign girl in the room with two hands full of thumbs.

My mother didn't take the insult lightly. From that day on, every afternoon after school I had to sit at the round wooden table in our dining room, across from the window that looked out towards the park and my happy playmates. There, I wrote rows and rows of each letter of the alphabet. I asked if I could write the Italian alphabet because it was shorter. Request denied. So on Mondays, I wrote letters A through G, and so on. Whenever a classmate phoned, my mother would look over at my hopeless script and shake her head no.

But misery yields to innovation, or at least to inspired thinking. I got so bored with writing letters, I decided to write stories. By then, thanks to my father, I was an avid reader in both English and Italian. Mom bought the idea, and I was off, finishing one silly tale after the next. It was so much fun, I'd write even more letters and words and finished early enough to head for the Rideau Canal with my skates in time to see the sun set over Chateau Laurier.

This very Italian concept of turning a mundane task into something creative and satisfying is part of moving the needle from ordinary to extraordinary.

Italians teach their children from a very young age to understand and appreciate the arts. This aesthetic enables them to step outside of themselves. More importantly, it engages the heart as a mediator between the head and the hand, so we work harder and with more joy and purpose. It makes everything click.

When I visited the Metropolitan Museum of Art with my Italian friend Alba and her ten-year-old daughter Federica, it was early morning, and we were the only ones in the sunlit European Sculpture Court. As we looked up at Canova's statue of Perseus holding out the head of Medusa, Federica said it was good that Perseus cut off her head because Medusa was a bad lady.

"Yes, Federica, and look at the irony. Medusa turned men into stone, but now her head is of stone," said her mother. Federica, with enormous hazel eyes and a head full of curls, laughed so hard she startled the sleeping guard. But we then launched into a discussion of Medusa's symbolic female power—the reason Gianni Versace used her face as the signature emblem of his clothing line. "He wanted to show the world that female sexuality is powerful because the woman owns it, no one else. How she uses it and expresses that power is entirely up to her. It's her right," said Alba to her daughter. Federica nodded. Even at such a young age she got it.

In the early renaissance galleries Alba discovered the Donatello, a bronze sculpture I'd walked past numerous times. As Alba described its movement and energy, the figure came to life for me. I saw the cherub's mischief in his eyes and the way his hand grasped away from his body. I knew he was up to no good. I finally understood, on a visceral level, why this was a masterpiece.

Federica told me that Donatello dressed like a pauper in spite of the Medici urging him to dress in a manner befitting his stature as Florence's most revered sculptor. He reputedly tossed his patrons' coins into the street for the beggars. Donatello's bronze David (now in the Bargello in Florence) influenced Michelangelo in a deeply personal way. It was the first nude sculpture since antiquity and considered one of the most powerfully erotic sculptures ever created.

A wooden sculpture of a Madonna and Child prompted a conversation about the transformative influence of Giotto. Alba pointed out that the flattened faces were a sign that this work was pre-Giotto and reflected the devotional, liturgical art of the Middle Ages. "The face of the child is almost an adult face," said her daughter. "The renaissance art faces were more human, like in Giotto's work. They look more like real people." At once, I felt I had a better understanding of how and why the art of the fourteenth and fifteenth century in Italy influenced all subsequent art movements well into the nineteenth century. It gave me a great sense of pride.

It was almost noon and we wanted to get to the *Manux x Machina, Fashion in the Age of Technology* exhibit before the crowds.

~

You know that feeling when something makes you stop and hold your breath because it is almost too beautiful to describe. As we entered the central cocoon of the exhibit, we saw the back of an haute couture wedding dress designed by Karl Lagerfeld. Its twenty-foot long train was hand-painted with gold metallic pigment, hand-embroidered with pearls and gemstones, machine-printed with rhinestones, and reflected in all its splendor on the domed ceiling above.

Inspired by the opening epigram of Fritz Lang's film *Metropolis, The Mediator Between the Head and Hands Must be the Heart*, the exhibit was a celebration of the immutable relationship between the hand and the machine in both ready-to-wear and in the traditional métiers of haute couture: pleating, lace making, leatherwork, embroidery, feather work, and artificial flowers.

I've always loved the French term métiers and the Italian *mestieri*. The names imply craftsmanship, a certain mystery and mastery, acquired through careful study and apprenticeships, emerging from a burning passion to make something of beauty.

A House of Chanel ensemble, a pink dress and cape made of silk chiffon and charmeuse, took me back to my childhood in Italy, to my mother's evening dresses on the Andrea Doria and the Vogue patterns she would cut and pin on the most exquisite fabrics she could find. Up close we marveled at the hand-embroidered pink silk satin flowers, pearls, and tiny pink-frosted crystals. The cape, decorated with the same pink-frosted crystals, was covered almost entirely with 1,300 hand-pieced pink silk satin flowers, hand-crafted by Maison Lemarie — one of the last Parisian workshops for pleating, smocking, and flower-making in the world.

I understood at once what John Ive, Apple's Chief Design Officer for *Manus x Machina; Fashion in the Age of Technology*, meant when he spoke about the symbiotic relationship between the hand and the machine.

"Both the automated and the hand-crafted process require similar amounts of thoughtfulness and expertise. Ultimately it's the amount of care put into the craftsmanship, whether it's machine-made or handmade, that transforms ordinary materials into something extraordinary."

I have walked the streets of Rome and Salerno with nieces and cousins half my age and younger. They can discuss the architecture and the history of their respective cities with the ease of a millennial using Snapchat.

They can talk about Beyoncé and Jay Z one minute, and later launch into a conversation comparing two of the world's most respected conductors, Riccardo Muti and Wilhelm Furtwängler. They know their writers, composers, designers, and architects. They marvel at sculptures, fabrics, fashion, and architectural detail. The palette of their interests and passions is vast and infinite.

This deeply visceral connection to the arts of every genre, whether classic or contemporary, is part of being Italian, wherever one lives in the world. It's as inseparable to an Italian's daily life, as are food, shelter, clothing or air for that matter. It's one of the key reasons why Italians always look so happy or, as filmmaker Michael Moore said in his documentary *Where to Invade Next*: "Italians always look as if they've just had sex."

I once heard the Director of Palazzo Strozzi say, "One should never walk away from a work of art unchanged." He nailed it. Every meaningful interaction with a work of art changes us. It forces us to slow down and see the world through a prism of different colors and angles. We let go of our fears and prejudices. We are forever transformed, determined to seek out the extraordinary in as many facets of our daily lives as we can.

EIGHT

THE DIVAS OF ITALIAN FILM

"Please don't touch my wrinkles. It took me so long to earn them."
Anna Magnani, actress

"I never felt scandal and confession were necessary to be an actress. I've never revealed myself or even my body in films. Mystery is very important."
Claudia Cardinale, actress

When you've emigrated from your place of birth, you know that one day, either by choice or necessity, you will be uprooted yet again. As untethered as that may seem, there is a point in your life when you decide it's okay. You become accustomed to a nomadic existence. You realize you can plant roots anywhere. It frees you from the fear of the unknown.

Too soon after my arrival, my beloved skating evenings in Canada ended full stop. We were about to become residents in yet a third country. My father had been transferred from the Italian Embassy to the Italian Consulate in New York City. No more twilight skates with my friends along the Rideau Canal. I so missed it. I missed the rink outside our school in Ottawa, with its log cabin in the center and the iron stove where we melted icicles off our mittens and drank real hot chocolate. I missed lacing up my skates on a whim to skate on the canal or even in a friend's backyard.

But then there was the Consulate on Park Avenue with its winding marble staircase or the sparkling lights on the trees outside at Christmas. Central Park with its skating rink and so-so hot chocolate was just two blocks away, and I could walk alone to the multi-tiered theaters in Times Square from my father's office to watch movies from a gargantuan screen. Back then, you could order actual tickets for special films like *My Fair Lady* and *West Side Story*, the little slips of paper arriving in tiny envelopes. Some films even had intermissions. And since so many movies were filmed in New York our enthusiasm grew with each new film. In fact, going to the movies was the tactic my parents used to make me excited about our new life in yet another North American country. It worked.

"There were years when I went to the cinema almost every day and maybe even twice a day, and those were the years between '36 and the war, the years of my adolescence. It was a time when cinema became the world for me."
Italo Calvino, writer

Oh for those long days in front of a tremendous screen, small hands shaking chocolate-covered ice cream bonbons out of a cardboard box! As kids, in the '50s and '60s, in both Ottawa and New York, we paid a little more than a quarter to watch film after film on a Saturday afternoon. Rainy days were a win-win for everyone. We got to go to the movies and our parents got us out of the house. The seats were far too big but super comfy. There were three tiers of seating, the highest level reserved for smokers and teenaged couples, who shooed us away when we tried to sneak upstairs.

There was a lot of excitement when the lights finally went out and behind us opened a small square portal from which beamed a blinding ray of light. We settled noisily into our seats and waited. A rattle came and the projector finally spun into gear. As the technician unrolled film, we watched the screen, concerned only with what was in front of us. Sometimes the film broke unexpectedly, the room became totally dark, and we'd yell until the rickety projector started humming again.

But whatever transpired, we knew that for those five or six hours we'd enter and exit multiple unexplored worlds. When we left the theater after five o'clock, it seemed as if an indeterminate amount of time had gone by. In concert with the characters of the screen, human or animated, we had lived days, weeks, years, odd experiences. We'd seen the streets of New York, the markets of Mumbai, the glaciers of Antarctica and the ballrooms of Vienna. We'd cheered, laughed, cried, and gone home chattering about the many countries we wanted to travel to and what we wanted to be when we grew up.

We watched Moses part the seas, James Cagney tap across Broadway, and Moira Shearer lace her red ballet shoes. We drooled over George Chakiris and the male dancers in *West Side Story*, and we tried to imitate Natalie Wood's eyeliner with a kohl brush from the local drug store. We didn't quite understand what plagued Joan Fontaine in *Rebecca*, but we knew Mrs. Danvers was evil and that the fire would destroy Manderley forever.

Leaving the theater was sometimes disorienting. One evening after watching *Moby Dick*, we stepped out into a wicked thunderstorm. Rain poured down in torrents and soaked through our clothes. Bolts of lightning streaked across the sky. We ran, terrified a giant whale might leap out of a back alley and swallow us whole.

After watching *Miracle on Thirty-Fourth Street*, we, en masse, harassed our parents to take us all to the Macy's Thanksgiving Day Parade. I believe my father scored multiple points in parents' heaven for agreeing to drive us. On one occasion during the slow drive through bumper to bumper traffic, I told him I wanted to live in an apartment on Central Park West when I grew up so that, if my children wanted to see the parade, all I had to do was direct them toward the window. And we could all watch from inside with mugs of hot chocolate and slices of panettone while the turkey and Italian-style stuffing roasted in the oven.

In a movie, there is a beginning and an ending that, especially in American cinema, pays off in a happy and orderly conclusion. At the movies we saw life played out in a way that made sense. It opened up our world and, for those of us new to America and to New York, gave context to our new lives. New York was not Italy and it wasn't Canada, but the movies made me think it was a pretty cool place to live.

Children like consistency, and films offered it through structure, aesthetic wholeness, and grand, archetypical stories. We were in good company in finding such pleasure. In his provocative memoir, *The Road to San Giovanni*, Italo Calvino recounts anecdotes about how he found solace in what was projected on the screen, an unreal world more unifying and ordered than real life.

"A different world from the one around me, but my feeling was that only what I saw on the screen possessed the properties required of a world, the fullness, the necessity, the coherence."

In our household, we distinguished among three categories of films. The Saturday afternoon movies, I saw only with my friends. Then came the nostalgic and often musical Million Dollar Movie or Early Show films of the '30s and '40s, shown for seven evenings straight on our black-and-white TV. Last, there were the films my parents and I had to travel downtown to see because they weren't showing in our neighborhood. These comprised foreign films and the newest technicolor American releases that opened up with an MGM logo and the head of a roaring lion.

For new American productions like *My Fair Lady*, featuring a prickly Rex Harrison and Audrey Hepburn in heart-stopping costumes by Cecil Beaton, we went to the large theaters in Times Square. We'd already seen the stage production with Julie Andrews and memorized the music and lyrics from the Lerner and Loewe record album my father gave my mother for her birthday.

One film I returned to see a second time was *West Side Story*. My father had been a great admirer of the conductor and composer Leonard Bernstein, who then lived in the Dakota building on the Upper West Side. My mother cited the dance sequences and the impeccable acting of Rita Moreno and Natalie Wood. Their characters, Anita and Maria, were two modern women finding their way in a new country, while casting aside the more restrictive traditions of their homeland. In Anita, my mother must have seen herself. She was the one who praised our new life in America, while my father spoke longingly of Italy. He was Bernardo, a romantic for whom Puerto Rico would always be home.

For the films by Italian or French directors, often shot in black-and-white, we took the subway downtown to smaller theaters in Greenwich Village. These weekly family outings included my father's detailed walking tour of New York streets settled by Italian immigrants during the early 1900s. A two-hour walk through Greenwich Village, the Bowery, Soho, and Little Italy yielded a trail of all the Italian-owned businesses and ended inside a legendary Sicilian bakery on Grand Street for a cassata Siciliana studded with dark chocolate chips.

To my parents, the post-film banter was a form of nostalgia. Italy at that time had no major film studios. The U.S. studios, which had consolidated in the 1920s, had evolved into thriving businesses. An

Italian film, by contrast, was less a production than an unembellished narrative set on location, a simple story told by a single writer, director, and actors on the stage of real life.

On one occasion, we met a cool young NYU student named Flavia. She was seated at the table next to us. I noticed her white Courrèges boots right away. They were popular at the time because of Marisa Berenson, the model and the granddaughter of Elsa Schiaparelli. I'd clipped every photo of her in *Vogue* and *Mademoiselle*.

Flavia introduced herself; she'd overheard our conversation about the Pasolini film we'd just seen. She was surprised and impressed that I'd see a Neorealist film at my age. I told her I didn't have a choice as my parents dragged me to every single one. They never censored any films. The only criteria was that it be a good film, versus a bad film, and if there was nudity or swearing or whatever the censors considered inappropriate, so be it. Flavia liked that. She also smiled when I told her I much preferred movies starring James Dean — I found Italian films depressing.

She said she understood, but that the neorealism genre was Italy's prolific response to the *telefoni bianchi* films of the Fascist era. Apparently these were inferior imitations of American comedies. They used Art Deco props, including white telephones, and stressed traditional family values, rigid hierarchies, and social convention. The neo-realists rejected the mimicry of set production in favor of authentic stories portraying the grim realities of post-war Italy.

What Flavia said made sense. While I hadn't fully understood what Anna Magnani had to do to save her son's life in *Mama Roma*, I knew it was something she was ashamed of. The raw emotion in her face made me sad for her, and the final scene, in which a plume of white smoke rises up in the distance, moved me to tears.

Whether through *Roma Città Aperta*, *The Bicycle Thief*, or *Mamma Roma*, I knew there was a part of my homeland we had been fortunate to leave behind, one that stood in sharp contrast to the sanitized and gossamer lives depicted in American films. Even so, while I loved to watch Fred Astaire twirl around a golden-haired Ginger Rogers, and although I admired Carole Lombard for her spirit, I felt disconnected from these potential female role models. Their lives had nothing to do with ours.

Flavia shed some light on that too. She explained that some of the most popular American actresses were so stylized by the film studios they didn't seem real, at least not to an Italian. There was the feisty Myrna Loy and a stoic Katherine Hepburn jousting with Spencer Tracy. They had flaws and dimension. At least that was an evolution of sorts. And I thought Katherine Hepburn, with her high cheekbones and tailored clothes, resembled my mother. But Jean Harlow was so white she looked more like one of my dolls than a live woman. And I had to admit the sheer number of blonde actresses in American films rendered them, at times, indistinguishable.

Italian actresses were anything but indistinguishable. They were fierce, dark-haired, and curvy, and for most of them, especially Anna Magnani, Sophia Loren, and Silvana Mangano, their first films were in the gritty neorealist genre. There was something genuine and tangible about these women. They exhibited a self-possessed and unabashedly sensual glamour. And since there were no studio systems or publicists to shape or mold their images, Italy's actresses established their images themselves — a bold and feral sexiness defined by women and not by men, a celebration of all things female including art, fashion, family, community, food, and wine.

As successful as they were, the divas of Italian film never renounced their Italianness — women like Silvana Mangano, who enchanted us through a sensual dance in *Riso Amaro*, or Claudia Cardinale, the wise and ethereal beauty in Fellini's *8 ½*, who spoke five languages and was named one of the fifty most beautiful women in film history. How I enjoyed seeing gorgeous Gina Lollobrigida ride on a Vespa with Rock Hudson through the Italian countryside. And how could anyone not revere Anna Magnani, the woman who enchanted Tennessee Williams and whose funeral at Santa Maria Sopra Minerva in Rome drew more visitors than the funeral of a head of state?

Aside from the gossip surrounding Sophia's relationship with Carlo Ponti, Anna Magnani's ill-fated affair with Rossellini, Silvana Mangano's divorce from Di Laurentiis, and other such stories, the divas led rather uneventful lives. They appeared at movie premieres and were photographed while shopping on Via Condotti or Cannes. But unlike their counterparts in other countries, they shied away from the limelight and the paparazzi to return home to family and friends. What they presented to the world was the impression of authentic lives fully lived, of fulfilling careers, glamour, travel, and luxury as a state of mind, not monetary privilege, alongside simple unembellished living and a strong connection to their home villages. And when Sophia and Gina did work in Hollywood, they clashed with producers who attempted to turn them into a Hollywood product. They would have none of it.

Finally, it was Sophia, Anna, Gina, Claudia, Silvana, and the inimitable Giuletta Masina who told me, from the screen, that there was something cool about being Italian. I wasn't blonde, and I didn't have neat little Wonder Bread sandwiches in my lunchbox; my father was not like Robert Young in *Father Knows Best*, and our last name had more vowels and consonants than a dictionary, but we had a culture to be proud of.

At home and in the theaters, we continued to watch both American and Italian films with great interest, but this time with three more discriminating sets of eyes, thanks to Flavia, who became a family friend and visited regularly, bringing pastries from the Lower East Side along with the latest film journals. American films were visually beautiful and entertaining, filled with hope and optimism. As we watched, we became transported. In our minds we dreamed, we laughed, we imagined all was possible, and each of us set out to make that happen, in whatever shape or context we defined. It was the '60s after all. America was prosperous. We had a handsome Catholic president and a stylish first lady who spoke French. The British had sent us the Beatles, the Rolling Stones, and Petula Clark. My hair grew long and my skirts were shorter, thanks to Mary Quant, and Mama didn't hesitate to dress me in what was new and trendy, whether my father approved or not.

Like it or not, the barriers between world nations had started to fall. And the arts played no small part in making that happen. Just as the Middle Ages in Europe had given up to the glorious Renaissance, just as the Renaissance ushered in the Age of Enlightenment, the restrictive 1950s fell away to new generations and a new order. Integration across cultures would happen. It would take time, but momentum was in our favor. As different as my two worlds were, the Italian and the American, I detected a common thread, a philosophical openness that told me the old world and the new one could and should co-exist, and that nothing could stop history.

So while my father shook his head when I would wait for hours at the Filmore East to snag tickets to a Jimi Hendrix concert, he would smile tearfully when I took him to see *Turandot* at the new Metropolitan Opera House in the then-futuristic Lincoln Center. This is where they filmed *West Side Story*, I whispered. Well, not here, but close by. With its red carpets, shimmery star-like chandeliers that rose and lowered before and after intermissions, and an open piazza over Broadway. The Met was not La Scala, but it was close.

NINE

TALISMAN OF HAPPINESS

"Food makes people happy, it takes you back home, it says so many things that words can't say."
Sophia Loren, actress

"Becoming American meant rejecting one of the two worlds. It meant trying to hide the grease stains saturating the paper in which your school lunch on crusty bread was wrapped, while the rest of your classmates ate ham on white bread with mayonnaise."
Maria Laurino, The Italian Americans: A History

My mother's favorite cookbook, *Il Talismano della Felicità*, was written in 1928 by the then high priestess of Italian cuisine, Ada Boni, who'd consolidated all those recipes Italian mothers and grandmothers of that era never wrote down. But Boni set out with a broader mission than just putting tosses and pinches into cups and teaspoons. She wanted to convey the complex history of the cooking in which every Italian takes pride.

This Talisman of Happiness celebrated all things Italian — art, conviviality, love of nature, and family — because Italian cuisine was never only about the food. Years before the food policy in Western nations went off course and Carlo Petrini's Slow Food initiative came to its rescue, the *Talismano* reminded us that cooking was about bringing people together to share good, clean, fair food — the true talisman of convivial happiness. To fully adopt the Italian approach to the preparation and the sharing of food was to transform the ordinary into extraordinary every day of one's life.

I saw its influences in how we adapted to our new surroundings in New York. After a few days, the initial shock of the American accent faded and I set off to make new friends inside our apartment complex in Astoria. Each of the girls was from a different place: Tina hailed from Greece, while Veronica was born in New York of Russian parents. Ruth's family was Jewish, her family worshipping at the Astoria Center of Israel, which my father told me had been registered in the National Register of Historic Places.

Our little Astoria was, even then, an enclave of ethnic diversity where we could access the foods of our homeland and sample those of others. Shopping in the markets along Ditmars Boulevard on a Saturday afternoon might yield a box of cannoli and napoleons and a second of baklava or rugelach. We could easily find fennel bulbs, grape leaves, broccoli rabe, and escarole in fat bunches for a few dollars.

At the art store where I bought my colored pencils, they displayed paint-by-number drawings of the Parthenon, a Venice gondola, a Dublin side street, and the Italian peninsula. Visiting my friends' apartments meant partaking in an Oktoberfest celebration, a Passover Seder, or an Orthodox Easter. The world began to open up, mostly through food and holiday rituals. But I still missed the Mounties and the First Nations People on their horses. Something else had changed. My mother decided to work. She announced it one evening over dinner, and the next day she left for her job at a factory in the garment district wearing a dress, heels, and lipstick. She was the only working mother in our complex. That sparked conversation, none of it favorable.

In both Ottawa and New York, our family formed loyal relationships with our local food purveyors. We bought our meats from a family butcher and ground it up ourselves for *polpette* (meatballs) or *polpettone* (Italian meatloaf). On any given evening there were three different vegetables of different colors served on our table. We bought daily bread from Alberto in Ottawa or Gino in New York, either in the form of a *sfilatino*, a crunchy baguette made from semolina, or a *pagnotta*, one of those round Tuscan loaves I had to carry under my arm.

It was the same bread my mother sliced thick and large for my school sandwiches. So while my classmates held neat little white bread triangles that smelled faintly of mayonnaise, I would self-consciously unwrap two huge oval slices dripping with olive oil from chunks of Italian tuna or a zucchini frittata inside.

As a working mother, Clelia had to set up an efficient system to ensure we ate well every day of the week. Frozen dinners, restaurant food, and fast food were out of the question. So every Sunday morning after church, we prepared meals for the week — tomato sauce, chicken broth, stewed lentils, minestrone.

My father stored a giant flask of wine in our closet, along with prosciutto from my uncle Minicuccio's farm near Sulmona. A friend of his at the airport smuggled it past customs. I loved my uncle Minicuccio. He had dancing blue eyes and full red cheeks. Not only did he know how to slice prosciutto at just the right thickness, he also made me chocolate bar sandwiches and introduced me to pecorino drizzled with chestnut honey.

What I loved most about my mother's meal planning on those Sunday mornings was the smell of tomato sauce simmering on the stove. To this day, making fresh tomato sauce from our own pressed and jarred-up tomatoes is my therapy for whatever life throws my way. Grab the crusty *sfilatino*, fresh from Bruno's. Break off a piece, dip it in the sauce, and eat. It's so delicious and so reassuring. You break up more bread and dip again, until mammina tells you to stop.

Many years later, on another Sunday morning when I'm twenty-six and have moved into my first Manhattan apartment — all five hundred square feet of it — I will smell sauce cooking in a neighbor's apartment across the hall. The walls are so thin, I can hear him sneeze. But this time, I don't say "God bless you." Instead I break off a piece of bread and knock on his door. His name is Lorenzo — a dapper third-generation Italian hair stylist who's just moved in with his partner, a Hungarian makeup artist named Lavente. They welcome me in.

Lorenzo gives me a bowl of sauce and more bread, and as I sink into a zebra chaise beside the iconic Milton Greene photograph of Marlene Dietrich, he starts to prepare the Bialetti moca pot. I smell the espresso beans that Lavente grinds. Lovely Marlene, dressed in black, is seated against an all-black background. She leans over to touch the back of her knee, and the light falls on her blonde hair and on her perfect legs.

As the espresso starts to rise and bubble, Lorenzo turns on a Mina CD. In front of me is the latest Italian Vogue with Marisa Berenson on the cover. I dip the bread in the sauce, and the three of us start to sing "Non credere." We know we will become (and remain) friends for eternity. We will create our own community of friends on the Upper West Side.

My encounter and subsequent friendship with Lorenzo might never have come about if not for Clelia's sauce and for her ingenious response to neighbors' criticism on one very hot July afternoon in Astoria. Our complex surrounded an inner courtyard that opened onto the street. Every afternoon and evening, mothers would set up lawn chairs to watch their children play. Three women in particular could be found seated outside at numerous intervals throughout the day. They'd watch the comings and goings of their neighbors, stirring a pot of gossip and spicing it up for attention like the good three witches of Macbeth.

My father did what men do so easily. He charmed them with a

smile. And being that he was so handsome, it worked temporarily. But he was not one to play catch with the kids in the courtyard or banter about baseball scores with the other fathers, so he remained an outsider and our family kept mostly to ourselves.

Clelia was about to change that. She prepared a special tomato sauce using olive oil from my cousin's *orto* (we'd smuggled that in, too) and the tomatoes we had mashed, de-seeded, stirred for hours on the stove, and jarred up ourselves. Just at that point when the simmering sauce released its most delicious fragrance, she opened the window.

The three witches looked up from their conversation.

She snipped the basil and bay leaf from our window box, uncorked red wine, filled a bowl with water and ice to keep cool the white peaches she and my father would slice up and put in glasses of wine. "When you're done," my father would say, "the wine tastes like peaches and the peaches taste like wine." My brother and I, meanwhile, put out biscotti she'd made that Sunday and arranged a platter of Italian pastries from Bruno's.

And what about the vehicle for the blessed sauce? Nothing was a more delicious companion than her *tagliatelle*, which she rolled out and cut by hand. Years later when pasta machines were all the rage, she still refused to use one. When you cut tagliatelle on the machine, you do so at the tips. When you cut by hand, you run the knife along the length of the pasta, rendering a porous surface for the sauce to sink into.

That afternoon, she had me make a salad with the freshest greens and tomatoes from a farm in New Jersey. We cut up fennel bulbs and put them in a bowl of ice. Then she walked outside, carrying a silver tray of iced teas in frosted glasses accented with our mint leaves. My brother, dressed in blue shorts and a white shirt, carried a bowl of white and red grapes carefully cut into bite-sized clusters. I brought the folding table.

The ladies were delighted. They commented on the unique taste of mammina's iced tea, made from actual tea leaves. They found the cold grapes luxurious. And then, gathering their children, they came inside for a feast. But it was more than a feast. While the food and its presentation were the draw, the true magic lay in the conversations the food evoked. A glass of wine, a forkful of pasta, laughter — through these we all reached out across the impenetrable wall that had kept us from connecting. Regardless of ethnic origins and quirky customs, we were human beings with the same concerns and challenges. As for our multiple differences, well, they deserved to be celebrated too.

Even though relationships with the three witches improved, I realized at that young age that mothers, especially working mothers at the time, were indeed subject to a different set of standards. My mother tried to put it in perspective. "No one has a right to judge you. You have to be true to who you really are. It's the only way to be truly and fully alive."

The night before I'd come across a similar line spoken by Marmee in Luisa May Alcott's *Little Women*. Her daughters Jo and Meg have just returned from a party where they had a great time until Jo overheard two neighbors gossiping about them. Marmee's response to Jo's frustration resonated in me then, as it does today.

"Nothing provokes speculation more than the sight of a woman enjoying herself."

Wow. Perhaps that was it. Regardless of what transpired within the walls of our small apartment, to our neighbors this stylish first-generation Italian woman exuded a different type of confidence. She was not afraid to celebrate her female self. She was not going to be defined by expectations that had no reason for being. And because of that, our little enclave would never be the same.

Less than a year later, other mothers in the complex went to work. Several women would ask my mother for advice on what to wear for a wedding or a graduation. She taught them how to hem a skirt without a single stitch showing. The three witches started to dress up more, and my mother bought her first pair of Levis. She, of course, tailored them to fit like designer jeans do today, hemmed at just the right length and worn with buckled ankle boots from Rome. During the holidays, we would give our neighbors some of our *croccante*, Italian nut brittle. And they would bring us those yummy butter cookies shaped like snowmen and Christmas trees, covered in sprinkles and icing.

In the evenings, when all the women came home from work, they'd gather together outside to talk. They were all, including my mother, having much more fun, and there was never a dearth of baby sitters or help with home repairs, car repairs, or speedy fixes.

So, whether it was enjoyment or survival instinct, there was no doubt that my mother flourished once she left the confines of her home province. We all did. Our ways were special but so were those of our neighbors, and the journey to extraordinary is all about navigating the ship through the fog of our own limited vision.

Little did I know that we were about to test those metaphorical waters yet again. No sooner were we well ensconced in our new community, my parents announced we would be moving.

"Vain trifles as they seem, clothes have, they say, more important offices than to merely keep us warm. They change our view of the world and the world's view of us."
Virginia Woolf

While my mother may not have read all of Virginia Woolf, she did hold onto a particular quote about style and dress. It was internal as well as external. It colored the way we saw ourselves. It brought pleasure into the daily task of dressing and stepping out into the world.

So on that frightful first day of fourth grade in my new school in the Bronx, I was, yet again, a foreigner in an Anglo-Saxon land. Five years earlier we'd left Italy for Canada, emigrated yet again to Astoria — and now to The Bronx, in New York City, where my classmates spoke an odd type of English and the girls wore pencil skirts and actual stockings instead of ankle socks. Everyone seemed so much more grown up. That made that first walk to the cafeteria one of the longest I'd ever experienced. One of the girls invited me to join them, but I'd forgotten my lunch at home and had no idea what to do with my hands or my words, so I retreated to a bench along a back wall by the window, not far from the lunch line where kids lined up, holding plastic trays.

As I stared out the window at the empty playground, wondering if I should make a run for it, I sensed a stir in the room. I turned to see my mother approach. The girls stared at her at first and then smiled. They whispered among themselves. Mama looked like a fashion model in her swirling skirt, patent heels, and red lipstick. She sat beside me, opened a pretty tin lunchbox. Inside was a panino wrapped neatly in paper, a thermos of soup, a small bottle of water, and an orange cut into small, even slices. I unwrapped each item, and as I ate, we talked, like two ladies out to lunch. She gestured for the still-staring girls to join us. When they did, she gave each one a tiny packet of sugared almonds tied up with a lavender silk ribbon, brought out of a soft leather purse, which the girls couldn't stop touching. "It was made in Italy," said my mother, and she let them look inside at the leather interior, the monogrammed letters, and tiny buttons and zippers.

They commented on her leather billfold, gold plated powder compact, and linen handkerchief with her initials embroidered near the tip. All at once, that foreign land I was born in became something exotic. Later that afternoon, my mother took me shopping. It was time for some grown-up clothes, she said: nylons, pointy-toed shoes "made in Italy," tailored skirts and frilly blouses — and a stylish satchel to carry my books instead of a schoolbag. I could tell she loved every minute of it.

TEN

FOOD IDENTITY

"One cannot think well, love well, sleep well, if one has not dined well."
Virginia Woolf, writer

In her opening statement in the Talismano, Boni dispels the pervasive belief that there is a single, generic Italian cuisine. Not so. Due to its late unification in 1861, Italy is as diversified in its regional cuisine as it is in its multiple dialects. It should be noted that the Italian word for country — *paese* — is the same as the word for town, indicating that each town held on to its own sense of identity, as did each region. You would often hear someone say she was not Italian but Venetian or Abruzzese. The sheer diversity of Italy's microclimates and the sea breezes along its peninsular coasts make each region's cuisine so distinctive that ingredients from other regions were once considered imported.

The plains and pastures in Italy's north are conducive to raising livestock and to the production of butter, cheese, and *salumi*. Pasta and rice in Emilia-Romagna are more likely to be prepared in a meat, cream, or butter sauce. I will never forget the tortellini in cream and sage at a restaurant in Parma's main piazza on a cool January afternoon.

The region's salty mountain breezes and autumn fog deliver

the perfect molecular ecosystem for our incomparable *Parmigiano Reggiano, Prosciutto di Parma,* and the most delicate *culatello* on the Italian peninsula. The pigs raised for the culatello are fed the whey left over from making the parmigiano, and the salty air and predominance of fog facilitate the optimal drying of both the prosciutto and the culatello.

Travel to the sun-drenched coastal towns of Liguria for fresh grilled fish and pesto Genovese made from the local herbs that grow wild there. Walk the trails of the Cinque Terre, and smell thyme and marjoram as you descend into Portovenere. Savor a pappa al pomodoro in Florence, a simple soup made from tomatoes, basil, oil and stale bread. You're more likely to have lots of beans and soups like ribollita than pasta dishes in Tuscany, and if you're going to order a steak anywhere, go for a Bistecca Fiorentina with a glass of Antinori's Tignanello. When you venture into the Tuscan hill town of Montalcino, try some *pecorino* with chestnut honey. And don't forget a splendid glass or two of Brunello di Montalcino.

In Milano, in the region of Lombardia, order a buttery risotto and a lightly fried cotoletta alla Milanese. In Rome, some spaghetti cacio e pepe, artichokes in herb oil and garlic, and a glass of chilled Frascati. The fertile volcanic soil in sunny Campania yields eggplants, peppers, salad greens, lemons, figs, and the country's sweetest tomatoes. I'm told that since there is no water in the soil the tomato plants have to reach very deep into the soil to get hydration. During the journey, they absorb all the soil's nutrients. That's why a tomato in Italy tastes better than it does anywhere else. Campania is also the regional home of mozzarella di bufala and limoncello.

So where in Italy do you find the best pizza? In the city it was created, Naples. In fact, Neapolitan food is considered, even by many of its northern neighbors, to be some of the best in all of Italy. I recently spoke with a Milanese businessman on the *Freccia Rossa* high-speed train from Rome to Naples. He told me he'd embarked early that morning on the first train from Milan so he could make it to Naples in time for lunch, because: *"A Napoli si mangia bene."*

The Sicilians might challenge that assumption. The rich volcanic soil of Mount Etna produces an abundance of lemons, blood oranges, almonds, and olives. This region's cuisine is unique in Italy because of its Greek, Spanish and Arabic influences. So be adventurous. Try the *agro dolce* (sweet and sour sauce) on your fish. And notice that the fish from the warmer waters of the Tyrrhenian Sea is different from the fish of the Mediterranean or the Adriatic, so the locals take full advantage and adjust their recipes accordingly. All the better for those of us fortunate enough to sample them with a glass of Corvo Bianco di Salaparuta in a picturesque villa in Taormina.

Some of Italy's tastiest food comes from southern regions, where its people have crafted ingenious delicacies from cheap, accessible ingredients: olive oil, capers, and red peppers. I will never forget the fresh figs I snatched from the branches of a tree in the summer of '69 or the glass of chilled Vermentino in Lecce after a swim.

Il Talismano, true to its name, did work its magic. Over the years, it answered every question I've ever had about selecting ingredients, preparing and serving food. It would define the flavors we sought to tease out of vegetables, herbs, meats, fish, and spices purchased carefully from our local grocers in three countries. It gave us the rituals around which we gathered and celebrated. And when we sought to branch out into new culinary realms, Indian or Middle Eastern food for example, it gave us a benchmark against which to ground our creative impulses.

In my adult years, when my husband Steve first joined us for the classic feast of the seven fishes on Christmas Eve, he was intrigued by my father's nimble way with fish. From the *Talismano* he'd learned how to buy, clean and cook clams, calamaretti, smelts, eel, shrimp, and to bring out their truest flavors. By the time each of the seven dishes came to the table, we had acquired a tasty and thorough education on the best ways to cook any type of food from the sea.

What intrigued Steve all the more was our post-dinner espresso political rants. These came about after all Sunday dinners and festive dinners, when we would linger around the table and talk in Italian. During one particularly heated discussion, he asked what we were arguing about. I replied, "Oh no, we are in total agreement."

I thank the *Talismano* for its reverence around all matters of the table. For my parents, it was yet another way to *fare la bella figura* whenever we had guests. First we ironed the linens, polished crystal and silver, set the table with flourishes of flowers and heirloom silver pieces. We did a full place setting, from appetizer fork to the tiny fruit knife placed horizontally in front of the dinner plate. We even had a pair of ornate silver scissors specifically designed to cut grape clusters.

And when dinner was over, there was the conversation over Amaretto as we cleaned up the glasses until they sparkled, polished the silver cutlery, and slid each piece back into its felt container. While our daily dinners were not as ceremonial, we still set the table with imagination and care, as if we were creating a frame for the stories and delights that would unfold around the table.

The *Talismano* taught us to embrace dining rituals of cultures other than our own. Finally, it reminded us that food, and the convivial rituals that surrounded it, did bring felicità in its truest form. But we were to experience the Talismano in all its magic that summer on our first return trip to Italy.

ELEVEN

JOY IN THE SIMPLE THINGS

"Open my heart and you shall see, Graved inside of it 'Italy.'"
Robert Browning, poet

"The power of finding beauty in the humblest things makes home happy and life lovely."
Louisa May Alcott, writer

This is where it all began to make sense. The mystique of southern Italy overwhelmed as we sailed into the Bay of Naples aboard the *Giulio Cesare*. I took in the gritty energy of the port and the outline of Vesuvius at our backs. My parents had said that everything was bigger and more vibrant in Naples. I knew the Neapolitan sense of humor was witty and layered with pathos. I learned this from all the Renato Carosone records my father played over and over.

I was told that Neapolitans sang in the streets. As a tugboat pulled the luxury liner toward the port and away from Vesuvius, we looked up at the funicular and the hills of the Vomero. Decades later, when I discovered the books of Elena Ferrante, I would wish we had not been greeted at the port by our relatives and so quickly spirited away. Instead we could have wandered streets in neighborhoods that reminded us of De Sica films, Sophia Loren, and the story of how the first *pizza margherita* was made.

At the time, however, I was only nine years old, my brother Umberto was two, and my baby sister Laura, eleven months. I'd lived with my family in Ottawa, Canada, then in Astoria, Queens, and The Bronx in New York. In five short years, we'd changed residences three times and schools, four. I'd kept acquiring new best friends and then leaving them to move somewhere else. I spoke English well, thanks to the excellent schooling in Ottawa. When the teacher asked the classroom where each of us were born, they gave street numbers and names from Canadian cities or New York boroughs. I had to say I came from Italy. The teacher would pull down the world map, hand me a pointer, and say, "Show them." She was more perturbed by their lack of geographical knowledge than my statement.

Even though I'd pointed out Europe as a continent and Italy as the country that was shaped like a boot, which they'd often seen on pizza boxes, I was still a foreigner. From a place that only existed in movies about Roman gladiators or gangsters in pin-striped suits.

They asked me why my ears were pierced and what my mother was saying when she spoke to me in Italian. Increasingly I'd wish I could wear clothes and shoes from the local stores, instead of the hand-knit sweater dresses and handmade leather shoes from Italy. And, as delicious as my sandwiches were, they looked nothing like everyone else's.

So perhaps this first trip back to Italy was a way of feeling we belonged somewhere, to a family tribe, if need be. However, I was unprepared for the crush of relatives and for the long drive to Rome, then on to Avezzano, where all my aunts lived.

I saw Naples in passing, a flurry of yellow, sky blue, and apricot neo-classical and baroque buildings. We visited the Piazza del Plebiscito

— named after the plebiscite that admitted Naples into the newly formed Kingdom of Italy under the House of Savoy — and had a *caffè affogato* at Caffè Gambrinus while a barista told us that Naples, founded by the Greeks, was named Neapolis, meaning new city, and was once part of the Kingdom of the Two Sicilies, ruled by the Bourbon kings.

In Avezzano, we stayed with my zia Antonina's family in a huge stone house on three levels with marble floors inside and wrought iron balconies outside. In the basement, she stored piles of grain, corn and almonds. This delighted my brother and me. We would climb up and slide down, or we'd settle in with a handful of almonds, cracking the shells with our teeth.

Then zio Pepe would come by on his Vespa and take me for a ride around Avezzano with a prerequisite stop for hazelnut gelato along the way, then on to my zia Natalina's *orto*, where she hoed the land from morning to night. Her fields seemed to go on forever, and I remember a particular night when I looked up at the sky and saw a single star twinkling. My zio Francesco raised farm animals and grew mushrooms, which he swore weren't poisonous, so I ate them by the handful.

When we weren't visiting one of my mother's six sisters and their families, we were at the mercy of the sarta Ivana, who made us stand still as she measured, pinned, re-measured, and yelled for us to stand up straight. We were told not to move, and if we did, the pins would pinch. My father and mother had suits made by the sarto next door, because tailoring was different from other types of sewing, and my father refused to wear anything that was not *Made in Italy*. For the entirety of his life, I remember a row of polished shoes, stuffed with shoetrees.

After our visit to the sarta and sarto, we made the rounds of the small artisan and family-owned retail businesses in Avezzano, a pretty city with small pastel-colored villas. My mother liked to peruse all the shops because they stocked merchandise of a quality one could not find outside Italy, especially with respect to knitwear and leather goods. With a strategic eye, she picked out our clothing for the next year, like flat-weave knit sweaters with raglan sleeves that were not sewn on, but hand-knitted in a stippled weave. Their colors came with evocative names: *ghiaccio*, or ice, a gray-toned ivory; bordeaux, burgundy; *grigio perla*, a pearl gray; and my favorite, *rosa antica*, an antique or dusty rose.

Mama showed me the hand-stitched lapels on my father's suits and turned my dresses inside-out to show how the seams were sewn first by the sarto or sarta's hand guiding the fabric under the machine, and then by their hand-stitching to finish off the fabric's edges. An industrial machine-stitch around those edges indicated an inferior product. "Always turn a garment inside out before you buy it," she said. "It should appear as clean and finished as the outside."

In the evenings after dinner, Clelia made us put on our nicest clothes and take a *passeggiata* in the *piazzetta*. Dressing up in the evening was a treat for my mother, for she got to show off her new outfits. Even though she repeated certain pieces, she never wore anything the same way twice. For my father, it was a chance to smoke a cigarette and drink an *amaro* or a *digestivo* with friends. And for my brother and me, it was all about gelato, two flavors topped with a dollop of *panna* and eaten with a tiny spoon. Umbertino usually dropped his, and so I had to share mine, which didn't matter because I could always ask for another. I remember how fresh and fragrant the air smelled.

"It's because of all the mountains around us," said my mother. "Abruzzo is the greenest province in all of Europe. We are in the center of the country and in the heart of the Apennines, surrounded by national parks and nature preserves. On a clear day you can see Gran Sasso, the highest peak, where I used to ski when I was younger." I heard the nostalgia in her voice. She did, too, and straightened her back as if to correct it. "We'll make sure to photograph it tomorrow."

If I'd wanted to know where my mother got her resolve, I had only to spend a week at nonna Laura's in my parents' home village of Antrosano. My mother and her sisters grew up in the largest and most imposing stone house in this small *borgo* tucked high in the hills. The house stood by a vineyard; a single twisting dirt road ran through the town center. On either side, other stone houses stood with huge wooden doors and wrought-iron terraces. Chickens raced and clucked as the occasional FIAT Cinquecento drove past, sending dust over everything.

I was drawn to laundry hanging on clotheslines as it blew about in the wind. And there was the frequent shouting from the balconies and along the streets, as children dressed in the classic black tunic and white-collared school uniform ran to catch up with friends or make it home in time for lunch. The fact that both boys and girls wore these tunic dresses was a surprise, but it also recalled something from a Fellini movie.

Since there was no running water, all the townspeople went to the *fontana* in the center to fill their enormous copper urns, one for drinking and the other for cleaning. So one morning, nonna Laura woke me from a bed that was so high up, I needed a stepstool to get down to cold stone floors. She insisted I wear her slippers. When I joined her in the drafty kitchen under the highest ceilings I'd ever seen, she ordered me to drink a raw egg. "You don't have eggs fresh from your own hens in America, Gabri, so how can you ever have strong bones?" To my horror, she chopped off the top of the egg and punctured a hole in the bottom. I wanted to die, but she put her hands on her hips, and as she stood over six feet tall, I drank it down, fast.

Surprisingly, it was cold and good, or at least not as bad as I thought it would be. But she was ready with a shot of Marsala just in case. She told me she would give me a dozen fresh eggs to sneak on the boat when we left.

Feeling lightheaded from the wine, I let her lead me out the door into the dirt roads of Antrosano. She balanced a huge empty copper urn on top of her head. Neighbors looked up from balconies and clotheslines to shout good morning or to shake rugs over the railing. Old men gathered around the only bar for their morning espresso. We passed Domenica's, the only place in town with a telephone, where the townspeople lined up every Sunday morning to make calls to relatives in America.

We were higher up in the hills above Avezzano, and from a ledge overlooking the valley we could see the snowy summit of Gran Sasso. Nonna Laura told me that soon they would build an *autostrada* to Rome and then everything would be simpler. The young people of Abruzzo would find work in the city and come home more often to see their families. "The young people all want to go to Rome," she said. "Your mother did move to Rome once. Her father made her come back. She should have stayed."

At the *fontana*, Laura filled the urn that, given its size, weighed more than the two of us together. She dipped in a ladle and passed it to me. "*Forza.* This is fresh water from our mountains and forests." It tasted clean and cold. I looked up and saw the glimmer of a tear in the corner of her eye. But in a second it was gone.

When the urn was full, she twisted a wet cloth into a tight circle on the top of her head, lifted the enormous urn, and pressed it down on top of the cloth where it sat firmly. She balanced it with both hands and started to walk back towards the house. She moved with the upright torso and core strength of a dancer. People stepped aside. Men tipped their hats, cyclists got out of her way. She paid little attention as a rabbit darted across the road.

She walked up the stone steps and I ran ahead to pull the door open. Inside, I smelled the fire burning, the lavender sprigs on her heavy wooden table at the center of the room, and the cold stone I will always associate with her house. Laura placed the urn on its pedestal not far from the fireplace and wiped the perspiration off her face with the wet cloth.

"It's not as hard as it seems, Gabri," she said, before dipping a ladle in to get a drink. "The reward you get is well worth it." I drank too. Water from *la fontana* was the freshest I'd ever tasted, cold and sparkling like a spring.

The townspeople had always known that Laura Di Cosimo was a woman to be reckoned with. Calm but strong, she earned everyone's respect. She had full control over her daughters, except for one, my mother Clelia. The problem with Clelia was that for her nothing was impossible or unachievable. If she couldn't afford a Schiaparelli dress, she would learn to make it. If her father denied her an education, she would buy the knitting machine, take lessons with the local sarta, and become proficient enough to earn her own money and move to Gianicolo in Rome.

Criticism did not deter Laura's daughter from walking to church in four-inch heels or from wearing wide-brimmed hats to shield her face from the sun so she wouldn't acquire the bronzed skin of a *contadina*. She wore lipstick everywhere. For her, it was a sign of feminine power, and the redder, the better. Digging through her purse, I would always find a lace handkerchief, a gold-plated pressed powder compact, and a lipstick, usually housed in a decorative refillable tube with a mirror on the outside. She sometimes carried a solid perfume in a ceramic compact.

What a delight in church, where I never paid attention, to click open the purse that still smelled of precisely tanned and scented leather, and pull out all these tiny tactile treasures to play with. I often wonder, if I had a grandchild today and she were to open my purse, what would she find? A cell phone and a small cosmetic bag filled with indiscernible plastic tubes and containers.

"Your mother Clelia has hands of gold," nonna Laura told me one evening, as she calmly rolled a ball of wool from a skein I held up between my two hands. She did this quickly, with swift twirls of her hand as the fire flickered behind us. "Whatever your mother touches, she makes beautiful."

I knew this then and I know it now. I know that when Clelia rolls out *sfoglia* for pasta, it will be as thin as parchment. I know she will insist we cut the tagliatelle by hand because they absorb the sauce better. I know that when the tagliatelle are finished, she will twist them into soft spirals. I know that when she rolls tiny meatballs for Italian wedding soup, they will be as smooth and flawless as marbles.

Because of nonna Laura, I now know more. I know that Clelia did go to Rome to the Ospedale Bambin Gesù, a children's hospital, not only to study nursing, but also to take care of her younger sister Lila, afflicted with polio. For Lila, Rome was terrifying; for my mother, it was liberation. She would take long walks around Gianicolo in the evenings, perhaps down that steep stone staircase where she walked many years later with my father. When they were in their seventies, I brought them back to Rome for their fiftieth wedding anniversary. It was their last trip to their beloved city.

But as a young woman alone in those wartime years, that walk was all about getting away to a less predictable and less secure place. So if I picture her now on that night, she would be sitting on those steps, smoking a cigarette and looking up at the stars. She would walk back up the long hill in the highest heels she owned and re-enter the hospital without waking a single person. She'd make sure Lila was tucked in and asleep.

Back home, a young woman was not allowed to walk alone at night. Here no one looked askance if she dressed and moved in that sassy way that garnered criticism back home. Rome was a place she where she could truly find her voice, at least until her father, Francesco, told her to return home. She was needed to help in the vineyard and to make some money through her knitwear so that all the girls could attend school. So when my zia Antonina's husband came to pick her up from the ospedale, Clelia was ready, dressed like a fashion model in a cloche hat and carrying a kidskin handbag from the Fontana sisters shop.

Girls from good families did not go to Rome, argued her father. Clelia closed the door to her makeshift studio behind the dining room, where she would continue to work on her knitting machine and turn out tiny outfits and caps for new babies, sweaters for her girlfriends, and British-styled cardigans for young men who stopped by sometimes just to flirt with her. She eventually married my father, and five years later they left Italy for Canada.

Nonna Laura's stories made me realize something else — that my mother had secrets. I didn't wonder then, as I do now, if there had been another reason she went to Rome, a lover perhaps, a Jean-Paul Belmondo type since she loved French actors, and I could see her with someone darkly intellectual like the characters he played. Did she sneak out late at night, take off her shoes so she could run down the stairs quietly to meet him in the shadows below Gianicolo?

I now know that all women have secrets, even our dearest and most intimate women friends, which is why they frustrate men. Men have layers. Women have facets: conflicting, sensual, passionate, and complex. There were parts of my mother I would never know. She'd guarded them with irrepressible joy. The extraordinary parts of herself, she would reveal on her own terms, or not at all.

So while I see in my mother many attributes of the stylish Italian divas she admires — Gina, Sophia, Virna Lisi, and her favorite, Silvana Mangano — I also see the hauntingly intelligent face of an Italian actress whom I feel best captures the essence of all women, their dreams, aspirations, and most profound secrets: the ever mysterious and influential Giulietta Masina.

Consider Masina's most magnetic role, that of *Cabiria*. In the final scene she looks at the camera without fully resting her eyes on it, without connecting with the spectator in any way. Only Chaplin had ever mastered this technique so brilliantly. *Cabiria* leaves us wondering what she has learned and what she'll do next.

TWELVE

A TRAVELER IN MY HOME COUNTRY

"When I went to Venice, I discovered that my dream had become — incredibly, but quite simply — my address."
Marcel Proust

"Gabriella, *guarda!*" My mother tugged at my sleeve and pointed out the train window at the stone towers of Castiglioncello jutting out over the sea. I remember the scent of pines and ilex trees and the hills spilling down to the inlets below. The castle turrets on that gray day looked like a setting for a Sherlock Holmes story.

My brother and I scrambled up on the wooden seats to stick our heads out the window, but the train conductor showed us the sign *Vietato Sporgersi* and made us sit down. We'd done this before, of course, at every train stop from Genova on up along the blue Ligurian coast, calling out to the vendors pushing carts of biscotti, beverages, and panini on the train platform as we waved a 500-lire note in hopes of getting the last pack of *quadrattini* — tiny multi-layered wafer biscuits with hazelnut cream.

The train guards spoke Italian, French, and German, logical since we were swerving wildly towards the Swiss border. Mama had packed panini caldi filled with frittata, nonna Laura's amaretti, and blood oranges from Sicily. We set up the train table with our own linens, glasses, and cutlery. I liked to watch my father peel an orange, like a sculptor. He'd rest the knife's edge at the top then peel all the way around on an angle. The cut was so even that when you pulled the peel away and held it in the palm of your hand, it looked like the intact orange. My mother was equally meticulous, only she cut off the tops and bottoms first, then drew vertical lines down the sides.

Later, we did go into the dining car for wine, water, more fruit, and deliciously smelly cheeses. We stared out huge windows at the flower-speckled countryside and doll-like villages snuggled inside mountain crevices. Church bells sounded every hour. Suddenly, the train dipped into a dark tunnel. As we emerged, my father told us to turn around. And there they were, pulling back behind us in all their jagged glacier magnificence: the Alps. They were so close at first and then pulled further and further away until I was finally able to see where the snowy peaks touched the blue of the sky. I held my breath. I felt the same frisson of excitement days later as we rode past the white marble peaks of Carrara, where Michelangelo sourced his marble. No matter how often one returns to a favorite place, it's like falling in love. There is nothing like the first time.

As a tourist in my own country, I wanted to capture all those firsts. We were to spend three months in Italy and Switzerland. I was missing school, but my teacher said I'd learn more traveling than in a classroom. She asked me to prepare a report of my travels, so I made a scrapbook where I glued in photos, journal entries, my drawings of piazzas and mountains, train tickets, dried flowers and herbs, and tiny Cinzano coasters. I couldn't wait to get back to talk about what I'd seen and show my ricordi (souvenirs).

In Florence, the colored marbles of the Duomo — white from Carrara, pink from Prato, green from Maremma — seemed to rise out of the shadows as we entered the Piazza del Duomo on bicycles from the narrow Via dei Servi. My parents bought me a Florentine clutch purse embellished with shimmery gold leaf and an imprint of the Tuscan iris sculpted by hand. We watched leather artisans sew the seams of handbags; other artisans engraved the same iris on leather bookmarks under a frescoed ceiling by Ghirlandaio in La Scuola del Cuoio, Florence's oldest leather school. And inside the Basilica di Santo Spirito, my mother showed me a small wooden crucifix by Michelangelo, so smooth it seemed to be made of marble.

Later that evening, we crossed the Ponte Santa Trinità across from Ponte Vecchio at sunset, the ideal moment to watch Florence's chiaroscuro light wash over the Arno and to sit on the bridge's stone railing, gelato in hand. Ponte Santa Trinità had been completely destroyed during the war. For many years, its sculptures of the four seasons lay at the bottom of the Arno until they were raised and replaced in 1958. It was rumored that the plans for its original design had been stored in a vault in the Uffizi, the elegant drawings and detailing suggesting the hand of one even so great as Michelangelo.

We took the train into Venice, and I watched the Campanile in St. Marco rise up over the lagoon. The idea of a city, a living museum, on the sea, comprised of tiny islands linked by bridges, seemed surreal, but there it was. We were constantly walking up pretty bridges over water, suspended, and then back down onto land again. I loved that sensation of being between two places, connected but separate, as gondolas sailed underneath.

We drank hot chocolate at Caffè Florian, crossed the Rialto bridge, chased pigeons in San Marco, and visited lace makers on Burano. They called Burano the island where the rainbow fell because of its colorful buildings. My mother bought a lace collar that she would affix to a Victorian-style red velvet dress intended for me for Christmas. In later years, I would remove it and attach it to a black silk shirt.

Tourism in Venice at the time was not as it is today. One could meander deserted streets and alleys without bumping into rows upon rows of stands selling postcards and t-shirts. On impulse, you could step into a stationary store or into an atelier selling engravings and authentic Venetian masks, then enter a large *piazzetta* by the Accademia and watch children jumping rope.

The black gondolas lined up by palazzi looked like musical instruments in repose. But at night, inside our hotel, the *gondolieri* would start to sing and we'd push open the very large windows to a view of the water, black and shimmering under a full moon, and knew this moment would define the floating city in our minds forever.

Venice, for me, will always be shrouded in mystery and music; Florence, in art; Rome, in architecture. There, in all three, and across all of Italy, the beautiful confluence of the eternal interlocking elements: art and life.

Years later, on a snowy December evening, my husband and I took the *vaporetto* from San Marco towards Giudecca. The fog was so dense that when we swerved away from the canal to dock, we couldn't see where we were. A gorgeous couple, she in red taffeta, he in a tuxedo, both wearing black capes, stepped into the boat. It was a scene straight out of a Zeffirelli film. We pushed out into the cold canal waters that sprayed over the sides of the boat. The couple barely noticed, the hoods of their capes fluttering under the full moon. Later, as we approached the dock, we heard music. The mist cleared and through the fog emerged the lit-up windows of a palazzo. We heard music and voices, and perhaps the clinking of glasses. The boat's captain helped the couple step out of the boat and off they went, capes swirling into the fog. To this day, I still wonder if I dreamed this.

Just as Venice's mystery burrowed deep inside our consciousness, so too the cinematic and sensual richness of Italy. Once one sets foot on Italian land, one is immersed in beauty, like plunging into an ocean one never wants to come out of. On the contrary, we want to lie back over its soothing water and float under the sun until it sets, all gold and lavender, and the stars appear. What I realized back then, as my heritage ignited all my senses, was how fortunate we were to be Italian.

While writing this book, I spoke frequently with my friend and fellow author Francesca Belluomini. We chattered on about our *caffè affogato* and prosciutto, sliced just right. About family traditions, about Campari and soda, and about our first pair of high heels (Italian, always). Most of all, we love that we are sharing our heartfelt love of our culture with others. It is about bringing them joy, as we knew it. According to Francesca, "What is ordinary under Italian standards seems a movie-set to someone who is not born under the same stars."

THIRTEEN

EXQUISITELY UNCONVENTIONAL

"What you wear is how you present yourself to the world, especially today when human contacts go so fast. Fashion is instant language."
— **Miuccia Prada, designer**

A woman who chooses to immerse herself in new experiences, smiling at life's perversions, exudes tremendous personal power. She is untouchable because she defies those who tell her she can't. And what better place to sashay that about than in the sassiest and sexiest of Italian cities?

I knew that my mother looked ravishing in the white gabardine swing coat she'd made herself. It swirled around her when she walked, and the barista at Caffè Sant' Eustachio near the Pantheon couldn't resist flirting with her. He ignored my father's scowl. The front of the coat swung around on a diagonal and buttoned over her left collarbone with a large mother-of-pearl square. Her pearl earrings matched the warm ivory tones of her ensemble, and her lipstick — Christian Dior Red.

She was, by far, the most stylish woman in the café, no easy feat in Rome where everyone looked like a film star. What's more, she knew more about the history of Sant' Eustachio, a Roman institution known to have a secret coffee recipe, than the barista himself.

But the best part was when we stepped out of the café and she pointed up at Borromini's dome of St. Ivo. Of all the church spires she had made us look at that day, this was one I liked most. She said it was a masterpiece of Roman baroque architecture and that we would be equally impressed by the church of Santa Maria Sopra Minerva, another masterpiece, but of the Italian gothic style. When they held the funeral for Anna Magnani there, the entire city showed up to throw roses on the coffin as it went by. "Was it because of her role in *The Rose Tattoo?*" I asked, and she nodded.

In the afternoon, we took photographs in front of the three fountains in Piazza Navona, tasted the real *tartufo* at Ai Tre Scalini, and walked up the Spanish Steps to Trinità dei Monti where my mother and I recited practically every line of dialogue from *Roman Holiday*. We later walked along Via Margutta and stopped at the gate that led into the garden and staircase where Gregory Peck had his apartment. The walls outside were of that rose and coral stone I will always associate with Rome.

Our city was working its cinema magic. So much so that the next pre-requisite stop was on Via Condotti at the store of Italy's shoemaker to the stars, Salvatore Ferragamo. My mother and I stepped into a virtual museum of *calzature*. Each shoe, like a solitary sculpture, sat on a shelf with enough white space around it so you could marvel at its shape and dream about slipping it on your foot.

Salvatore Ferragamo was more than an artisan. Borrowing from the renaissance principle that art and science are interconnected, he'd studied anatomy so he could make shoes that were as wearable as they were beautiful. One could imagine dancing in them. In fact, Joan Crawford did, all the way to a hundred dance trophies. And I'd imagine Judy Garland did so as well, in the rainbow wedge he designed for her to celebrate the iconic song that only she could sing with such heart in *The Wizard of Oz*. Today, if you visit the Ferragamo Museum in the Palazzo Spini-Feroni in Florence, you will see the handmade wooden lasts for the feet of Ava Gardner, Audrey Hepburn, Marilyn Monroe, Sophia Loren, Joan Crawford, and many other film stars.

"Let's buy an apartment in Monte Mario and come here every summer," proposed my mother later, as we re-grouped at the Caffè Canova Tadolini, once the home and studio of the neoclassical sculptor, Antonio Canova. Another handsome and quite flirty barista prepared an *espresso corto* for my mother, just the way she liked it. *"Te lo offro io,"* he said. The Italian way of saying it's on me, but a common gesture of hospitality, especially when there's a certain chemistry between people. I looked from one to the other. There was no mistaking the attraction, and my mother enjoyed it immensely.

Art surrounded us in the form of the sculptor's muscular preparatory models. Lots of statues of "handsome nude men," noted my mother with her characteristic mischievous smile. I wanted to return to the conversation about moving to Rome. I was already imagining an apartment on Vicolo di S Maria in Trastevere, or something along Via Margutta, or on Gianicolo, or somewhere close to my favorite *gelateria* in Monti, but yet another barista, Giovanni, became smitten with my mother, and my father asked for the check.

Clearly Clelia was having fun with my father's, or anyone else's, discomfort. Even then, before the word feminism entered our vernacular, she was unabashedly self-aware. For her, there never was and never would be a conflict between femininity and feminism. Nothing was to interfere with appreciating beauty and acknowledging her own vibrant, sensual female self.

My mother's badassery at the time is a part of the Italian woman's playful and perverse wink at convention. It calls to mind the iconic visionaries of Italian style, among them Elsa Schiaparelli who infused her designs with the irony of the surrealists and gave a voice to gutsy women everywhere.

In 1930, Schiaparelli's first evening dress, a simple black sheath and a wraparound blouse with white sashes, both in crêpe de chine, sent shivers up the spine of the fashion world. Elsa didn't care. She had set out to break the rules and was quite happy that her irreverence did not go unnoticed.

Decades later, Miuccia Prada would upend the concept of evening wear altogether, saying that the combination of a beautiful woman in a beautiful dress didn't interest her. Why not wear heavy wool for evening dress, a tiara with a sweater? "Tiaras are like wearing hats with diamonds."

Tiaras would not have been enough for Schiaparelli, whose tragicomic connection to the Surrealists found a voice in her work. She created the first true hybrids of clothing and art, a collection of exquisite cocktail hats shaped like high heels, a lamb chop, and a vagina, collaborations with Dalí that included a white evening gown decorated with a bright red lobster and worn by Wallis Simpson to celebrate her engagement to the Prince of Wales. By 1940, Schiaparelli had already revolutionized the way women dressed, inventing wraparound dresses, culottes, the jumpsuit; swimsuits with a built-in bra and the unforgettable power suit; and even the V-shaped broad shouldered jacket and pencil skirt worn by Marlene Dietrich and Joan Crawford. She delighted us with fun furs, camouflage prints and plastic clothes.

Both Schiaparelli and Prada, born six decades apart, were ardent rebels and feminists, who'd entered their métiers during times of social ferment in the arts and politics: Schiaparelli influenced by Man Ray, Duchamp, and the modernism of Edward Steichen; Prada by the demonstrations and radicalism of the '60s and '70s. Their mutual disdain for conformity refuted the archaic Pygmalion paradigm of fashion. They weren't concerned with prettiness or with social convention. And while other designers preoccupied themselves with designing clothes for women to please others, Schiaparelli and Prada set about dressing women who only wanted to please themselves.

Today, we hear these echoes in the voice of Franca Sozzani, the late trail-blazing editor of Vogue Italia. For Sozzani, who pushed the limits of avant-garde fashion journalism, the images inside the magazine had to be more than beautiful. They had to have context and meaning. Stories, photographs, and editorial content required a frame, as in a film by Fellini or Antonioni. They also had a purpose, to reach out into the bigger world and bring awareness to important issues. Like her predecessor Schiaparelli and her contemporary Prada, Sozzani saw fashion as a force to empower, not restrict women.

She was not the only one. Throughout history women, especially public figures, have used dress to assert their power. One example is Princess Diana, who wore a stunning black, pleated chiffon dress designed by a little known Greek designer Christina Stambolian to a *Vanity Fair* dinner in 1994. The media went wild. And not only the paparazzi. Hours earlier, in an unprecedented television interview, her husband Prince Charles publicly admitted he was having an affair. The sight of a plucky Princess Diana striding into the gallery, only a few hours later, in a figure-hugging off-the-shoulder dress and towering Manolo Blahnik heels rendered her victorious. The Revenge Dress, as it was called, announced the Princess's strength and independence — and her intention to use her title and power for philanthropic work on the world stage.

Then, when Michelle Obama greeted the Italian Prime Minister Matteo Renzi and his wife at her final state dinner at the White House, she wore a dress of rose gold chain mail designed by Donatella Versace. The first lady, a master of the art of political dressing, chose the dress for two reasons. In the name of sartorial diplomacy, it acknowledged Versace as a prominent name in Italian fashion. But more importantly, she wore it only one week after her magnetic speech about female empowerment in New Hampshire. Its selection delivered an artful and subliminal message about female strength and the power of self, a message reinforced later that month by Ms. Versace, who described her women's wear collection being shown in Milan as "all about a woman's freedom: freedom of movement, freedom of activity, freedom to fight for their ideas, freedom to be whomever they want to be."

I believe that was the very spirit I saw my mother express at the café on our last afternoon in Rome so many years ago. Her choice of dress, setting and demeanor were not about decoration. They were set inside a frame. They had context and meaning. We were to fly home the next day, and Clelia was determined to live those last moments in the Eternal City in the most extraordinary — and the most Italian — way possible.

FOURTEEN

PIECES OF HOMELAND

"Travel is the enemy of prejudice, bigotry, and small mindedness."
Mark Twain, writer

Travel as much as you can and as far as you can. That became my philosophy after that first return trip to Italy. Travel changes a person forever, and when I returned to New York, all my apprehensions about being foreign had vanished.

But amazing me most: I had suddenly gained popularity — not by rejecting my culture and language but by embracing them.

Friends who'd questioned my pierced ears and long name now wanted to know everything about my trip. What was it like to cross an ocean on a luxury liner like the one in *An Affair to Remember*? Did you get seasick? How were the kids in Italy? How did they dress? What music did they listen to?

Did you see Sophia Loren? And wow, those earrings really are cool. Did you buy them in Rome or in Venice or in Florence? You are so lucky your ears are pierced. I like your new shoes. How fab that you got your hair cut in Italy. You look like one of those Italian actresses with short hair and the tiny spit curls all around. I like the way you do your eyeliner. Do you really speak Italian? Say something.

I shared pictures I'd taken with my father's camera, using up countless rolls of film. When we had over four hundred pictures developed, my father looked at the bill and asked if I thought he was president of Kodak. I'd taken photos of every monument, café, side street, piazza and fountain. I took photos of young Italians on their *motorini*, of a gelato with three small scoops of *gianduia*, *stracciatella*, and *bacio* topped with *panna*, of stylish women in heels riding Vespas, monks carrying briefcases across St. Peter's Square, Fontana di Trevi at sunrise when I was the only one there to toss a coin in, and little boys in white-collared black smocks running to school. I took pictures of my six aunts, some of their husbands, all my cousins bunched together, and of my beloved nonna Laura, standing tall in her vineyard, hands clasped at her waist. In another photo, I held a *grappolo* of fat, red grapes in my hand. Behind me, stretch rows of vines to her peach-colored house with its terra cotta roof on a hill surrounded by poplars and pines.

Looking at the photo of the house, I could almost smell the damp stone, the fire embers, and her minestrone in a large cauldron on the stove. I smelled the carrots, onions, zucchini, celery, tomatoes, bay leaves, and cannellini beans simmering and blending together into something distinctively hers. Everything came from her garden. Everything was chopped and thrown into the pot by her muscular hands. In my mind, I retraced my steps along the cold stone floor in my bare feet, her shouting at me to put on my slippers, toward the huge front door that I could barely push open, and then down the winding dusty street past Domenica's house and toward the wide-open view of Avezzano's church steeple, Gran Sasso, the soothing sky of Abruzzo, and the soon-to-be built autostrada to Rome. I could never capture that in a photo. I had to smell it and feel the earthy breezes on my face.

Those photographs and memories made it easier to answer my schoolmates' questions. They wanted to know if the pizza in Rome tasted the same as it did by the Ditmars subway stop where, at the time, Gino charged fifteen cents for a slice. I had to explain that pizza was prepared differently in other regions of Italy. My favorite was the Neapolitan variety because it had a raised outer crust while the center was very thin, and the tomatoes were just about the best I'd ever tasted.

When we lined up to play dodge ball in the courtyard, the boys asked if I'd learned any soccer kicks while in Rome. Given my lack of athletic prowess, they already knew the answer. So I told them that I'd seen my uncles Peppino and Francesco bounce soccer balls off their heads in Italy. That got their attention, but I still didn't get picked for either team. I contented myself with being a runner, picking up stray balls that flew over the low railings onto the pathways outside.

In the 1950s, few Americans could afford to travel abroad. Our family was fortunate because the Italian Consulate paid for our crossings. Otherwise, a five- or ten-day sailing cost thousands of dollars. With air travel limited and equally costly, only the wealthy could afford to see Europe.

The popular film *Sabrina* shows the once down-to-earth Audrey Hepburn, a chauffeur's daughter, return from Paris as a stylish diva. In *Three Coins in a Fountain* three young women fall in love in Rome; throwing coins in the fountain, they are promised they will never leave Rome or they will be forced to return if they do. At the end of the film Louis Jourdan, David Niven, and Rossano Brazzi appear by the glittering fountain, the song plays, and the city's romantic image is fixed in everyone's memory. When I see the film today, I think of the *gelateria* to the right of the fountain where I have sent friends and family members over the years. No one knows the name of it, but the purveyors make some of the best *gianduia* and *caffè gelato* in all of Rome.

The fact that our family traveled frequently outside the country made us exotic, and since we regularly invited my friends and their families in for Christmas and Easter sweets or for mama's homemade pasta, we became everyone's friends. My parents rejoiced when anyone came to visit. I understand more clearly now that they were trying to maintain a sense of community for my brother and me, and that this community was ever growing. Unlike many of our immigrant friends, we had no family in North America. My brother and I had no uncles, aunts, or cousins until we boarded yet another ship of the Italian line to sail back to Italy where obscure family members appeared en masse.

Growing up this way, we never missed the extended family dynamic. By extending our Italian hospitality to friends, we created a different type of community, one which blended both worlds into our own. In the U.S., one talks about having company or dinner guests. In Italy one says *ricevere gente*: we receive guests like gifts into our home. I believe my friends felt this, so kept returning. The journey from ordinary to extraordinary starts with a full acceptance of one's self.

Embracing my culture, I made my mother take me to The Hatbox beauty shop to cut my hair even shorter, à la Lollobrigida. It had to appear just so, not like the overly pouffed imitations I saw in the pages of *Mademoiselle* and *Seventeen*.

Even such a short time in Italy had given me a trained eye. I knew to pare back, when a hair or dress style didn't work, if the skirt length should have been longer or shorter, if an outfit merited a touch of heel, if a red lipstick would suit an outfit more than the Cover Girl candy pink I bought at the drug store.

I also donned the traditional filigreed pierced earring look seen on my nonna Laura, my aunts, friends, and cousins — a tiny bauble dropped from a thin gold loop, a blue stone in the center. The swirled detailing mirrored the renaissance design on my leather notebook from Florence.

Looking back, I'm grateful to my parents who, while embracing our new country, did not try to make us assimilate into what some called the American melting pot and others called a mosaic. They acknowledged the opportunities this new life would afford us and respected the laws and practices of our adopted home. But Italy had a heritage to be proud of. It was our native land and we were never to forget that.

So at home we only spoke Italian, and outside we were to speak English correctly without slang, without dropping our g's or giving any disrespect to the language of Dickens, Austen, Luisa May Alcott, and Henry James.

FIFTEEN

TURNING SAUCE INTO SASS

"There is Garbo, Dietrich, Monroe, and Sophia. Who else inspired the whole range of feminine charms, from sex to motherhood?"
Lina Wertmuller, filmmaker

On the evening of April 9, 1962, when I was sixteen, there was a major ruckus in our living room. My father yelled, "Brava!" and popped open a bottle of Asti Spumante. Sophia Loren had won the Oscar for Best Actress in Vittorio De Sica's *Two Women*. The award, for whom the nominees included Audrey Hepburn, Piper Laurie, Geraldine Paige, and Natalie Wood, was presented by Burt Lancaster and accepted by Greer Garson. Sophia was in her apartment in Piazza d'Aracoeli in Rome, where she and Carlo Ponti lived. She'd chosen not to be in Los Angeles for the awards ceremony just as Anna Magnani had decided five years earlier.

It was a long night. With the time difference, they would not hear until early the next morning. So Sophia did what so many Italians do when we are anxious. Make sauce. The smell of tomatoes simmering in olive oil, onions, and garlic, after she'd peeled, diced, and thrown everything into the pot on the stove, took her back to Pozzuoli, to her nonna Mama Luisa, the matriarch who'd inspired her willfulness and dedication.

When the sauce was done, she and Carlo settled in and waited. Shortly after six thirty that next morning, she received a call from her dear friend and devoted admirer, Cary Grant. He told her, with great emotion, that she'd been awarded the Best Actress award for her spot-on portrayal of Cesira in *La Ciociara* (*Two Women*).

Sophia, whether acting in drama or comedy, got under the skin of every character she played on screen. She considered Alberto Moravia one of Italy's finest writers. So when the director Carlo Ponti told Sophia he was thinking of buying the rights to Moravia's novel *La Ciociara*, she read it from cover to cover in two days.

In her biography, *Yesterday, Today, and Tomorrow*, she tells how this book changed the trajectory of her career and her life. It validated who she was and her personal history. Because even though Sophia, the actress, had been to Paris, London, Hollywood and Cannes, even though she had starred in films directed by Cukor, De Sica, and De Laurentiis, and acted alongside Marcello Mastroianni, Cary Grant, and Toto, she was, in her heart, Italian. She was still Sophia Scicolone, born in war-ravaged Pozzuoli.

The unusual story of how a very young Sophia Loren earned the role of Cesira speaks to the collaboration of four women: Romilda Scicolone, Anna Magnani, Sophia Loren, and Eleonora Brown. George Cukor, the director, had chosen Anna Magnani to play the mother and Sophia as the daughter. Magnani, called Nannarella by her colleagues, refused. Sophia was too imposing a presence to play a vulnerable, teenaged girl. When Cukor insisted, Magnani told him to give Sophia the role of Cesira. Cukor dropped the project, but De Sica took it on and knew exactly what to say to a reluctant Sophia. She argued that she was not a mother and much younger than the character in Moravia's novel. But Vittorio reminded her that the role of Cesira was not unfamiliar.

In courage and cunning, Cesira was none other than her own mammina Romilda. Now all Sophia had to do was what she'd done with every prior role she ever played. She needed to summon up the courage to get inside her mother's head when they were hiding from the Moroccan soldiers. She would have to find within herself that maternal instinct for survival that makes one think quickly and without a second's hesitation. And she would have to feel the raw anguish of a mother whose only daughter, still a child, had been so brutally violated and is now forever changed.

The role at once became personal, and even more so when De Sica cast as her daughter the thirteen-year-old Eleonora Brown, the child of a Neapolitan woman and an American. Since Eleonara was so young, Sophia immediately became both nurturer and mentor. She felt responsible for this shy and intelligent young girl who would, in the role of Rosetta, place all her trust in Cesira. With such a powerful impetus, Sophia channeled all the maternal love she had felt as a child to Eleonora, and from that emerged one of the most powerful performances of her career.

For Sophia, *Two Women* was the painful story about her land, about the bond between mothers and daughters, about the war and the wounds it left behind. Now it all laid bare in the pages of Moravia's *oeuvre*.

"*Two Women* broke my heart. In those pages I recognized the courage, hunger, and blind stupidity of bigotry and the ignorance that were part of the war, as well as the redemptive maternal instinct that thrives in every woman everywhere."

But perhaps, for Sophia, Moravia's novel was an affirmation of what Italian women knew long before the philosophical arguments of the Neorealists, Dwight Eisenhower's warnings about the military-industrial complex, and the films of Dalton Trumbo: War takes far more than it gives. Industrialized nations had yet to embrace the full range of war's economic advantages, but they moved in that direction. Then, as now, women did not have a place at the table where such decisions were made. Consequently, once war broke out, they summoned whatever power they did have and, to great effect, fixed what was broken and mitigated further damage.

Two Women was one of the last films in the Neorealism genre. As Italy started to regain its economic footing and optimism, filmmakers introduced more entertaining and lighter fare, Italian comedies featuring Sophia Loren and Marcello Mastroianni and the famous spaghetti westerns. Antonioni and Fellini… Italy on the Tiber began to resemble Hollywood, even as newer and younger filmmakers took divergent paths.

One filmmaker in particular, Lina Wertmuller, would direct a new breed of films about war, the working classes, and the impoverished people of Southern Italy. With razor-sharp irony and searing insight, Wertmuller fashioned darkly humorous stories around Italy's Communists, anarchists, and anti-Fascists. In 1975, her internationally acclaimed *Seven Beauties* earned four Academy Award nominations, including Best Director. Wertmuller was the first woman nominated in that category, followed years later by Sophia Coppola (another Italian), Jane Campion, and Kathryn Bigelow. Significantly, in 2010, Kathryn Bigelow did win the coveted Oscar for *The Hurt Locker*, based on a true story about the Iraq war and the recruits who lived it through multiple tours of duty. Once more, a woman had lifted the curtain, taken us backstage behind the theater that war has become.

SIXTEEN

INTERCONNECTED FASHION

"In a machine age, dressmaking is one of the last refuges of the human, the personal, the inimitable."
Christian Dior

"Fashions fade, style is eternal," said Yves Saint Laurent. The valuable lesson of our Italian culture, imparted every day, was that style was not something one purchased, but a philosophy one lived. That philosophy was grounded in a keen sense of connection to the sources of our food and our clothing. We knew where things came from and what it took to get them there. We wanted to dig in our hands as we did with fabric, planting soil, and pizza dough. Pre-packaged, quick access, easily disposed of items had little appeal. They lacked the tactile qualities we thrived on. They lacked life and provenance. They were easy but forgettable.

Or as fashion expert and author Francesca Belluomini says so eloquently, "A noteworthy moment cannot be mass produced."

During my college years, Clelia grew even more capable and confident in her sewing. She graduated from *McCall's* and *Butterick* to *Vogue* patterns. She experimented with different techniques: pleats, tucks ruching, smock stitch. And she taught me how to blind stitch a hem with a gentle but firm hand.

With any garment, it was all about three things: the fabric, the fit, and the finishing details. My mother was particularly fond of mandarin collars or anything that made her think of the Orient. She loved the silks and brocades, the vivid colors, especially Chinese red. My father would argue, in his conventional way, that serious women didn't wear red. I now understand that this was vernacular for chaste versus unchaste women, but at the time I just thought he was being silly.

My mother didn't listen to him or to anyone else. She made red silk blouses to wear with her beige linen skirts and added wide belts to her dresses. We would flip through the pages of *Vogue*, tear out photos, and draw the changes we might make to a designer's sleeve, collar, or cut. Then it was all about that trip to the fabrics departments at Macy's or B. Altman's. Those departments no longer exist, but at the time they were weekend excursions of such joy I never wanted to end.

Imagine walking in between aisles upon aisles of gorgeous fabric: textured, embroidered, beaded or polished; silk, satin, brocade, shantung, or crêpe de chine. Just the cottons alone — piqué, eyelet, dotted Swiss, polished cotton. And then the wools — gabardine, ottoman, wool crêpe, tropical wools. Imagine the intertwining of colors and textures: bordeaux velvets, whisper pink silk, celadon and rose brocade, aquamarine chiffons, and snowy white linens. My mother knew them all on an organic level. To hear her describe a swath of champagne shantung silk was to receive an education on the source of the fabric, its cultural provenance, its weaving method, and all the glorious possibilities for its interpretation.

How I miss those stores and those days we spent together. It is yet another piece of old New York that we've lost: a connection to the raw material, the workers, the science and the craft. In a culture of fast fashion, we lose those relationships and the visceral satisfaction of interconnectedness. Fabric felt alive then, as did the story of its progeny.

More than anything, I miss that process of engagement from start to finish when you first unroll the fabric—a *tabula rasa* not unlike a blank canvas approached by a painter or the empty page in a journal before you pick up your pen to write. You have no idea how it will turn out, and that alone sets your heart racing. You look through magazines, you stare at women in the street, and you flip through the patterns until you find the one that's the *coup de foudre*, as the French say. Love at first sight. And then it begins, and continues, until that final moment when you slip the dress over your head, fasten its buttons, and stare into the mirror.

Clelia and I once came upon a textured French cotton in celadon and cream. The celadon pattern set against a creamy white with bluish undertones was all the more striking. This would be a dress, cut at the waist with a gathered skirt. We would puff out the sleeves a bit and have them end just below the elbow with a ruffle. Or a subtle lace trim. Or a high neck and a wide belt that snaps in the back. We found the lace trim and braided cord for the belt and collar. Via my mother's practiced hand, the dress came into being and fit perfectly, but it was the colors that enchanted. The only other place I'd seen that shade of celadon was in a Japanese vase at the Metropolitan Museum of Art.

Then, there was the New Year's Eve outfit. It was the 1970s when Barbara Bach's face graced the cover of *Seventeen*, Twiggy's style was still the rage, and the magazines' pages featured sequined boleros, satin blouses, and dirndl skirts. Time to break away from the old and move on to the new. My mother and I found a thick cotton-backed velvet in candy pink for the skirt; for the bolero, a silk fabric embroidered in silver thread and pink sequins. We paired these with a pale pink satin blouse, a silver and rhinestone chain belt, and glittery silver stockings.

When YSL introduced the wide bias-cut skirts and silk charmeuse blouses tied in billowy bows at the neck, Clelia replicated the look. It was right after the designer's exuberant Ballet Russes Spring/ Summer collection in 1976. He commented that he didn't know if it was his best collection, but it was certainly his most beautiful. The show reminded me of the First Nations People with their brilliant colors and headdresses. Yves was giving us another part of the world; just one year before he launched *Opium* and the sumptuous Chinese evening ensembles in the 1977 Fall/Winter collection. He'd introduced us to dress as costume, something we, as lovers of theater and film, had always known. Fashion — like a film set, a novel, or a painting — could transport us to the steppes of Russia and as far away as the splendid temples of Chinese emperors. As Diana Vreeland, curator of the YSL exhibition at the Metropolitan Museum of Art, aptly said, "He is the master of the streets of the world. All of them reveal and radiate his style."

In 1966, Lee Radziwill, sister of First Lady Jacqueline Onassis and a fashion icon who favored French haute couture, turned to Milanese designer Mila Schön to design her dress for what author Gloria Steinem called, "The Party of the Year" — Truman Capote's Black and White Ball in the Plaza Hotel's grand ballroom. This graceful silver-sequined evening dress worn under an equally sumptuous quilted white silk coat caught my mother's eye. She loved its simplicity — how it flowed over the body in such a flattering way, sparkling like so many stars on fabric. It would be impossible to copy it, but why not construct something similar?

So, in my freshman year of college, for our annual Snow Ball at the Crystal Room in Central Park, Clelia made me a long white and silver brocade gown with a matching cape-style coat and white faux fur trim. It had no sleeves, only slits on either side, so I had to wear white elbow length gloves that closed at the wrist with mother of pearl buttons. We found a small clutch purse covered in cultured pearls, and the effect was complete. In a circular all-glass room lit by crystal chandeliers, I felt as if I'd walked onto a film set in just the right costume.

Our collaborative sewing projects connected with the seasons. Every spring it was the hunt for an Easter outfit, which had to include a hat and gloves. Each fall and spring, we would look through *Glamour,* *Mademoiselle,* and *Vogue* to pick out fashions to copy. The year Cybil Shephard and Cheryl Tiegs appeared in tartan, lace, and velvet on the fall magazine covers, my mother made me a red tartan skirt and black velvet vest with silver buttons. We found the ideal ruffled lace blouse with a Victorian collar. We didn't need to buy a cameo since we'd purchased one in Naples. Add black tights and black chunky shoes, and the look was complete.

Jackie Kennedy's A-line dresses were fresh, inspired by Courrèges and a snap to copy, and we had great fun shopping for pillbox hats, swing coats, and clutch purses. It was not unusual for us to leave our Bronx home at nine o'clock in the morning and return after six pm at night without stopping for lunch. But how could we resist? In those days, Fifth Avenue and its 34th Street offshoot was a fashion paradise bordered on both sides of the avenue by grand luxury retailers: B. Altman's, DePinna, Bonwit Teller, Franklin Simon, Arnold Constable, and the Bootery, where I bought my first knee-high boots, mimicking the Carnaby Street look of the Beatles' girlfriends Jane Asher and Patti Boyd.

In 1960 in Italy, Irene Galtizine, who'd presented her first entirely Italian collection at the Sala Bianca in Palazzo Pitti, introduced the timeless tunic and trousers look. Working with brilliantly colored shantung silk from a Como silk manufacturer, she fashioned a minimalist design and embroidered the neckline and cuffs of the tunic. Diana Vreeland, the then fashion editor of *Harper's Bazaar,* baptized the look *palazzo pajamas.* Who wouldn't want a chic outfit that felt as comfortable as a pair of pajamas? Palazzo pants continue to intrigue me to this day. I adore them.

This promise of effortless, comfortable luxury enchanted Jacqueline Kennedy, Elizabeth Taylor, Audrey Hepburn, Claudia Cardinale, and Monica Vitti. It enchanted my mother, too, so she made, and I still own, a row of tunic and palazzo-trouser outfits, one in a vivid rose and silver-trimmed Thai silk that I've re-purposed over the years. One could say I have a vintage shop within my closet, a treasure trove of imaginings.

Season after season, Jackie Kennedy, Audrey Hepburn, and Marisa Berenson remained our staple fashion icons. We followed Claudia Cardinale, Sophia Loren, and Monica Vitti, and the writings of Diana Vreeland in *Harper's Bazaar* and Anna Piaggi in *Vogue Italia*. We wanted whatever they wore. These women exuded gravitas and independence, the badass attitude of the '60s. They understood style was not about labels or social standing. It was a way of life. It required an understanding of the world and its inhabitants, and it annouced an understated grace that informed one's choices. As they were generous of spirit, suitably cultured and multi-lingual, my parents considered them good role models. Their attributes, like the lovingly designed garments of those years never have and never will go out of style.

SEVENTEEN

Risks are Possibilities in Disguise

"The life you have led doesn't need to be the only life you have."
Anna Quindlan, writer

L iving an extraordinary life involves risk. Risks are possibilities in disguise. We invite these risks in as our longings urge us to. The only thing to stop us is fear. So, if while pursuing your dream, you find yourself on the precipice of something scary, there's a reason you got here — and every reason to keep going. Because nothing is worse, or more ordinary, than a life without magic.

One December evening, I found myself yet again, inside the Crystal Room at Tavern on the Green in Central Park. This time, I wasn't a college student but a young working woman at a business event. The only constant was my dress, made by Clelia based on a Dolce and Gabbana ad in *Vogue Italia*. I stood in front of the reception line because I'd been hired by Clinique Cosmetics as the Director of International Training, and on that night, the opening reception for our annual meeting, I would meet my global team for the first time.

They'd flown in from Europe, Asia, Africa, and Australia. They represented numerous countries and the multiple talents women bring into a business due to their ability to think outside the box. Many had been with the Lauder companies for years. Each brought a unique facet to the whole, whether through cultural insight or sheer inventiveness. It was, for me, an overwhelming moment. I had landed what many considered a dream job.

And my Italian-American influences played no small role in getting me there. In my mother's lexicon, you had to find a way to channel your interests into work you loved. And if, for any reason, it didn't deliver on its promise, you had to figure out a way to make it do so. In short, you had to go about the business of transforming the ordinary into extraordinary.

In my father's world, you looked at the arts and the sciences for guidance. There were life lessons in Shakespeare and Dante, in Da Vinci and Marie Curie, in the musicians of the Jazz Age, in the essays of Oriana Fallaci, and in the Italian-inspired architecture along Central Park West. So whatever programs or strategies you put in place, make sure to draw on the arts for inspiration.

And in my future husband's pragmatic American mindset, there were solutions to every problem. Success was a journey, not a destination. And failures were to be welcomed as moments of learning, stepping stones along the way. One simply had to dispense with self-limiting fears. It's true I knew nothing about the cosmetics business, *but what an illustrious challenge,* he said. *Yes, you love your current job because it's comfortable, but why not shake things up?*

Given that energizing pep talk, I was well equipped to leave what was comfortable and move on.

But it wasn't easy. When the offer first presented itself, I was in a great place. In fact, I could not have been happier. I loved my job, my colleagues, and the 1940s New York feel of my surroundings. At around the same time, Steve and I moved into a spacious pre-war apartment off Columbus Avenue. Memories of my Ottawa home, Thanksgiving Day parades, and my parents' ongoing love affair with Manhattan meant that Steve and I would live on the Upper West Side for many years.

We were both drawn to the brownstone side streets, the parks, and sidewalk cafés reminiscent of a European capital, and the overall laid-back feel of what was then a bohemian and affordable neighborhood. With manageable rent, we were able to afford the occasional dinner out, off-Broadway plays, even trips to Italy via hostels and discount airlines. We made use of free parks concerts and street fairs, shopped for bargains on Orchard Street, made frequent trips to my parents' Bronx neighborhood for groceries at a fraction of Manhattan prices, and cultivated a great group of friends from all parts of the city and its boroughs.

My brownstone office, overlooking St. Patrick's Cathedral on the other side of the park, felt like an extension of home. It was all so cozy. And then the call came. A headhunter invited me to interview for the position of International Training Director at Clinique Cosmetics, a division of the Estee Lauder Companies. In my new position, I would oversee training and education in all our affiliates, and be in the position to hire and develop my own team.

It sounded perfect, especially as it was international, made use of my languages, and involved the fields of fashion and cosmetics. I received a great deal of encouragement from my ever-supportive husband, even though the job would involve a significant amount of travel. He knew it was the right career move for me. I was reluctant. I was riding on a wave of success. And he said the one thing that changed my mind: "You've set it all up. Now it can run on its own. You're too young to be a maintainer."

How apropos that this event would be in the Crystal Room. Designed entirely of glass, the Crystal Room extended from Tavern on the Green's stone building into the park outside. Clinique's colors, echoing those of the setting, were green and white with silver accents. We dressed the space in white flowers with trailing vines, slid a silver napkin ring around each napkin, and placed a silver Clinique compact and lip brush inside tiny gift bags.

A waiter in a black tuxedo carried a silver tray of champagne. We sprayed our signature scent, Aromatics, and walked through it. Although our corporate colors did not incorporate black, black was the fashion color of the night, in velvet and taffeta, sometimes accented with white, often studded with pearls — and always uncompromisingly chic.

Clinique's founder, Carol Phillips, a former *Vogue* editor, had launched a brand that promised to make skincare and makeup regimens more manageable for busy women. The iconic Clinique ad showed the three simply packaged products next to a glass with a toothbrush. Since my two prior careers, educator and writer, had nothing to do with cosmetics, I had to learn the art and science of marketing. I had to look at my role in an entirely new light.

My humanitarian tendencies had always directed me to lead with the intent to empower others. That, in turn would benefit the company, I knew. But it was not enough. In my new role, I now had to weave in a brand marketing strategy and grow a business. I was determined to balance both priorities. At the time I had no idea that this self-imposed, humanistic business model was so closely tethered to my Italian heritage.

I believe in signs however, and I got one. That night in the glittering Crystal Room, just as I thought it could not be more magical, it began to snow. As large flakes covered the park, the streetlights went on, as did the lights braided along shimmering white tree branches outside. Candles flickered on the white tables, the chandeliers sparkled brighter than before. This was my own romantic entry into the world of cosmetics.

EIGHTEEN

STYLE IS AGELESS

"True beauty in a woman is reflected in her soul. It's the caring that she lovingly gives, the passion that she shows, and the beauty of a woman only grows with passing years."
Audrey Hepburn

Miuccia Prada once commented, "Age is the prison women make for themselves." The Italian and Italian-American women I know refuse to step inside that prison. I'm thinking of one in particular whom I was fortunate enough to meet at Milan Malpensa airport only two months after our glorious evening in the Crystal room.

Luisa Cacciatore, the Italian Training and Public Relations Director for Clinique, was close to my mom's age, in her mid-sixties. Wearing Missoni, bronze ballerina flats, a silver fox coat, and the truest red lipstick I'd ever seen, she announced, "I love who I am. Deal with it."

The General Manager of the Italian affiliate was a Swiss gentleman named Hans Thalman; he rode his bike into the office every morning and gladly deferred to Luisa for all matters related to training or public relations. Luisa checked me into the Hotel Palace and took me to the Galleria for a welcome caffè, *a cornetto*, and my very first glass of blood-orange juice. I feasted my eyes on the gothic spires of the Duomo and let her speak.

Within a few minutes, I learned about all of Luisa's life philosophies. She had a keen sense of the cosmetics and fragrance business throughout Italy and relished representing the Lauder brand, which she described as *un amore*. Over the next few weeks, we would visit, and I would work in, the small family-owned perfumery shops in Parma, Bologna, Milan, Florence, and Bergamo. I would form life-long relationships with the families who ran these small artisanal businesses. I even got to work in Profumeria Aline in Florence, one of the most elegant perfumeries in all of Italy. I loved that each fragrance was showcased in a traditional crystal flacon with a long, quilted pump. It felt so luxurious to hold it in the palm of one's hand, lift the pump, and spray a perfume mist behind each ear. I felt like a movie star.

Luisa traveled with me as an onsite mentor, carrying a small suitcase packed with knits that traveled well because they didn't wrinkle and only two pairs of shoes. She packed light and well. Style was all about simplicity, color, and comfort — there is no style without comfort, and playful coordinated colors took away the guesswork. There were lots of women at the helm of these family businesses, she said, like Estee Lauder. They had their finger on the pulse of a multi-faceted, multi-tasking female consumer. They knew that beautiful could also be practical.

Luisa was watching her diet as it was the end of January and bikini season would soon arrive. She liked to take the sun in May before the crowds. As she ate her cornetto slowly and with satisfaction, she told me that her diet was as simple as everything else. It consisted of cutting back on wine and bread. That made sense. I thought of my friends subsisting on cottage cheese, diet sodas and carrot sticks, and drew the conclusion that we simply overdo it in the States. I looked around me at women enjoying their food and wine, even the occasional gelato or *aperitivo*, with great joy and without guilt. Inspired by Luisa, I did the same.

In Parma and Bologna, we savored the delicacies of Emilia Romagna:

Prosciutto di Parma sliced at just the right thickness, creamy chunks of Parmigiano Reggiano, tortellini in a light cream and sage sauce, and peppery greens dressed with olive oil and lemon. It was too cold for gelato, but not for *semi freddo* or a piece of good dark chocolate. We opted for both. I deprived myself of nothing. I didn't count calories or carbs, and on the rare occasion when I skipped a glass of wine at lunch, I made up for it with a glass at dinner.

Like my mother, Luisa displayed the same lack of food guilt. Eating healthily with attention to one's *linea*, or figure, did not mean deprivation. On the contrary, one became all the more discerning. That meant tastier, smaller bites of whatever one had a desire for. On a particularly gray afternoon, under a dense fog in Milano, Luisa had a craving for a *cioccolato calda*. She knew of a bakery in Brera, not far from the Pinacoteca, where they served a very thick dark hot chocolate and the *panna* was always fresh. I remember that she held the cup in her hands and smiled before taking the first sip.

"Do you know what this reminds me of?" She went on before I could answer. "My nonna Angela, who is no longer with us, but she lived in the Valtellina, a valley near Switzerland in the north of Lombardia. When I was small, I would watch her melt the chocolate on the stove so slowly until it was like a syrup, and I would stick a piece of bread inside because there is nothing better than bread and chocolate." I told her my nonna would make chocolate too, especially on cold nights. I liked it better than chamomile tea. "And did she run a hot metal box over your sheets to warm them up?" she asked. "Oh yes, it was the oddest thing, but when I got into the sheets they felt so warm." I thought then of the cold marble floors in my aunt's house, and I began to miss that Italy, Laura's small humble town so far from the majestic architecture and fashion prominence of Milan.

"I miss the Valtellina," she said, sipping more chocolate. "Remember when our grandmothers would draw water from the fontana and roll out pasta by hand with a wooden broomstick?"

I described how my nonna, too, went to the fontana and that my mother still rolled out her pasta with the same broomstick she'd used when I was a kid. Luisa squeezed my arm and told me I was fortunate I still had my mother; she'd lost hers when she was twenty-five. I was lucky, too, that she'd taught me to eat and dress *all' italiana*.

"It's not that we're better," she said, re-applying her lipstick without looking in the mirror. "It's that you should never forget who you are. Your heritage is a part of you, like your eye and skin color. It's deeper and more significant than you know. As you grow older, you will want to get even closer to your roots. Some day when you are fifty years old, you will no longer want all the material things that matter so much to you now. You will want, more than anything else, to gather those you love for a simple meal, a glass of wine, and lots of laughter. You will applaud everything your Italian parents gave you. And besides, who does not want to be associated with *Made in Italy*? We Italians make the best of the best in everything. The world is starting to notice."

Mealtime conversations moved fluidly from business topics, which she handled with aplomb and decisiveness, to politics, on which we both disagreed, to discussions of fashion, with her describing the style ethos of each Italian designer. I took notes. And finally, to the longest conversations of all: food.

She was born and raised in the north, so her preferences skewed in those directions, even though she confessed that nothing compared to pizza in Naples, especially in those small *trattorie* near the port. The Sicilians, she noted, also knew how best to season fish, and even though she realized I rarely ate meat, she implored me to try the roasted pig in Sardegna.

"They dress it in myrtle, which grows wild there, and cook it inside a deep stone oven. You also must try their liqueur, *Mirto*. But it's best to drink it in Sardegna, where you are surrounded by the wild beauty of the place. It's a different kind of nature. It's rough and raw, and after a few minutes it enchants you. I would never drink *Mirto* in Milan. You have to drink it in the place they make it and have that setting around you."

She told me how she drank a glass of warm water and lemon every morning, then went for a swim or a long walk. "They say angels whisper to you when you are walking. It's when I get my best ideas."

We talked about our favorite things to eat for breakfast, what we craved when we traveled, and the guilty pleasures we could never resist. With every meal and in every restaurant, I felt like I'd been invited into someone's home. In spite of its grand architecture and the persistent buzz of its fashion industry, Milan does have an intimacy in select places, especially in tiny restaurants along I Navigli.

Luisa knew the owners, never looking at a menu but asking simply for what was good that day. On one particular day, the chef recommended a sea bass baked inside a thick salt crust. The preparation, he explained, was simple. He would slice open the *branzino* and sprinkle in the herbs. Then he'd close it and cover it with a thick layer of sea salt that hardened when baked. The sea salt did not absorb into the fish, rather sealed in its moisture and allowed for deeper penetration of the herbs. When the fish was ready, he chipped off all the salt to show us. He drizzled first-press olive oil, sprinkled a bit of parsley, and that was it. Simple and perfect. "All in the ingredients," said Luisa, touching the sleeve of her gabardine jacket. "It's like fashion. You start with the best material, and then it's about the fit. Simple is always better."

With that in mind, Luisa became both mother and friend as we prepared to shop the boutiques along Via della Spiga. It's worth noting here that this was a time when high-end designer wear was far more affordable and accessible than it is today. Prices were lower, the exchange rate with the U.S. dollar was favorable, and I became adept at reclaiming VAT tax at the airport. So, armed with those advantages and knowing we had a few hours before the drive to Florence, we went to Krizia, Versace, and Genny.

Since I'd explained to her that my mother had been a *magliaia*, the first stop was Krizia for some of the coolest knitwear I'd ever seen. Krizia's founder, Mariuccia Mandelli, had introduced the fashion world to hot pants in the 1960s, and was then making long tunic sweaters, short dresses, and thick scarves. With Luisa's guidance, I purchased a few pieces that I still own and treasure; they look as fresh and stylish as they did then. I treasure them all the more after Mandelli's death in 2015. The same is true of a silk shirt with a high neck and deep ruffled cuffs, designed by the departed Gianni Versace.

Donatella Girombelli is still alive but is not designing as much as she did when Genny became my go-to fashion label, thanks to Luisa, who introduced me to her graceful feminine clothes. On that first trip, I purchased a terra cotta blazer, a silk blouse, trousers, and a lovely lavender and white polka-dot dress in chiffon with a matching jacket. I still own the dress and jacket. I knew then, as I know now, that when I put on a Genny dress, I feel extra special. Each time I'm back in Milan, steps from the Galleria and the magnificent Duomo, I remember Luisa and hot chocolate, and her tutelage during my first few years in the field of cosmetics. I remember a vibrant woman who taught me that growing older was no excuse for giving up on style, good food, joyful living, or oneself.

NINETEEN

ROMAN HOLIDAY

"Whoever runs toward the future while forgetting their past mislays their identity."
Nicoletta Spagnoli

E ven jetlag couldn't tarnish the moment. I'd flown in that morning. My room was not yet ready; didn't matter. I settled in at a poolside table of Hotel Gran Melia. My eyelids started to close, but I was jolted awake by the joyful sound of a cappuccino and a dish with a cream-filled cornetto placed on the Carrara table in front of me. I looked up at the umbrella pines of Rome.

I was at the base of Gianicolo, where my mother had made her first foray into the Eternal City as a young girl. The Ospedale Pediatrico Bambin Gesù, now world-renowned, sits high on top of the hill by the statue of Garibaldi. Down below the hotel, in one of the labyrinthine streets of Trastevere, is the bookstore I visit year after year. If I look out and up I see the walls of Castel Sant' Angelo on the other side of the Tiber. On that day and forever, Rome would feel like a movie set.

I bit into my cornetto. The crème anglais oozed and tasted as delicious as the cream my mother and I would stir on the stove in Ottawa. Guests leapt into a blue pool. The apricot stone of the hotel quarters surrounded branches of mimosa and bougainvillea. White

108

umbrellas rose over tables where guests lingered quietly, and I wished Clelia could have been there so I could tell her she was the reason I'd come; why I'd developed this hybrid life of mine.

When we explore our heritage, via intention or impulse, we make unexpected connections. They come to us while we read a line in a novel or watch a mother roll up the sleeve of her child's sweater, when we catch a whiff of jasmine on a summer evening in Villa Borghese or rub a fabric that rustles the way it did when we were children.

We taste it in the *frutti di bosco* miniature strawberries you can't find anywhere on the other side of the Atlantic, even though you've searched every farmer's market in New York State. The connections insinuate themselves at whim. They couple and uncouple, but always in those moments when you can't use your cell phone because of roaming charges and you yourself want to roam, without a plan.

Later that morning, I walked alone into the wandering *vicoli* of Trastevere. I took in the morning smells of espresso from the tiny bars and the chatter of people going to work. The zip of a young woman on her Vespa, sunglasses toward the sky. The newspaper stand where my father and I, and years later Steve and I, would pick up both the *International Herald Tribune* and the *Corriere della Sera*. We'd fold them both under our arm, and off we'd go to the closest bar for our morning caffè latte.

In our household, it was unacceptable that we wouldn't know what was happening outside the borders of Italy, Canada, or the U.S. Every event, large or small, on any continent, had a rippling effect on all of us. When you're a child, the thought that your world could be impacted by someone you'd never met, in a country miles away, was perplexing at first but then made sense. You'd read about it in books assigned to you for summer reading, or inside pages of your World History or Earth Science textbooks, where the interconnectedness of world events, ecosystems, and cultural practices felt organic and logical.

Our geography teacher would give us world maps to color, and empty plastic capsules, like the ones medicines come in. We were to fill the capsules with whatever products grew or were produced in certain parts of the country on the map. We filled capsules with cotton, olive oil, pine needles, and apple seeds. It was a way of connecting us to the earth and to where the pieces of our life came from.

So that morning, I walked along lungotevere to recover some of those sensations. After many visits over the years, I'd expected that at some point my love of the city would wane. The opposite happened. I slid hands into my pockets and hummed a song by Nilla Pizzi, one of those languorous Roman ballads that lament the changes in this eternal city. I knew it was corny and the changes were real, but for me Rome would always be Rome. Its *fascino* was as immutable as the stones of the Colosseum.

A half an hour later, after a brief stop at Isola Tiberina, this small island in the middle of the Tiber, I continued along Via del Corso, Rome's main artery, past Piazza Venezia with the Forum beyond in search of the one pair of shoes that would make my heart race. But nothing caught my attention, at least not in the *calzature* department. I instead, focused on Rome's architecture, sunlit colors of its stone, its baroque, renaissance, and gothic facades, the breezy gait of stylish Romans on their way to work or to lunch past a backdrop of centuries old palazzi.

I had been in Rome so many other times, I could no longer count them. Rome had figured in my life journeys over and over again: a beacon that reminded me I once intended to live here. My mother has always wanted to live here. Steve adored the city too. So what were we waiting for?

I walked briskly until a white knit tunic inside the window of the Luisa Spagnoli boutique stopped me mid-stride. It was made of *lana d'angora*, with a voluminous collar. Its sleeves ended at square-cut mother-of-pearl buttons on the cuffs. The mannequin wore it with white merino leggings, tan lace-up ankle boots, and a bronze cuff bracelet. Each contemporary piece finished with a single old-world detail: a braided motif around the cuff; a hand-knit border, rather than a machine hem, hugging the ankle of the leggings just above the boot.

Roaming charges be damned. I called Clelia, who, at ninety-two, still worked at a beauty spa in midtown Manhattan. She would undoubtedly be in the coat checkroom, wearing her immaculate black-and-white uniform, the symbolic red door pin over her heart. Her hair was recently colored and styled, her fingernails manicured.

"Gabri, che bello, come stai, mama?" She always calls me mama even though she's the mama. It's an Italian thing.

Since the ensuing conversation warranted another stop, I settled in at La Buvette, one of the most Roman of coffee shops. I describe the dress in detail. She loves that it's white—my best color, she says. I know I wear too much black. With my olive skin, it drains. "Nero fa piu vecchia," she reminds me. "Black makes us look older." I do agree that black was far more flattering on me in my thirties than it is now, but it's the spine of my NYC wardrobe and a throwback to all my years in the fashion and cosmetics industries.

Still, I couldn't deny that the white knit made one dream, the way the best Italian fashion, regardless of price point, always does. Astonishing without astonishment. Uncontrived. Effortless. You knew right away that it was Italian. The word *respect* came to mind.

When we'd arrive home after shopping in the fabrics department at B. Altman's, my mother would lift a virgin fabric from our shopping bag, wrap it around her hand. "*Bisogna rispettare*," she'd say. It was an affirmation of a wise choice, as well as an allusion to the process ahead. As a knitter, she knew the magic lay in the weave, in the threads of the cloth, the smallest elements of the finished product. She'd make the sign of the cross before putting scissors to it. And now she's telling me to respect my good eye. "Buy the tunic, Gabri. You'll never find anything like that here."

She also reminded me that she knitted the angora coat and cap

I wear in my childhood photo in 1953, aboard the Andrea Doria, from skeins of *L'Angora Spagnoli*. Before our sailing, she'd traveled to Perugia to buy as much of the wool as she could afford. She knew she'd never find it in North America; its properties were as coveted as gold, created via a method that was entirely cruelty-free long before the term existed.

TWENTY

LUISA SPAGNOLI, TRAIL BLAZER

Luisa Spagnoli was born in 1877, in the medieval city of Perugia, home to Giovanni Pisano's splendid Fontana Maggiore, the University for Foreign Students, and the dramatic Via dei Priori. Surrounded by Etruscan and medieval walls, Perugia sits on one of Umbria's green hills. Lake Trasimeno is close by, as is the miniscule town of Panicale, known for its amber-lit piazza and summer concerts under the stars. Whether Luisa Spagnoli ever walked the paths of Saint Claire and Saint Francis, or visited the towns of Gubbio and Assisi, we will never know. We do know she loved the land and the traditions of her home province, intending to preserve them through all her future business endeavors.

A feminist ahead of her time, she anticipated the integration of women in the workforce by fifty years. Through her creativity, leadership, and relentless hard work, she founded two major Italian companies: Perugina and Luisa Spagnoli. Through them, she birthed a chocolate empire and put the Umbrian textile industry on the map.

Before establishing that business legacy, the young Luisa ran her father's apothecary and pastry shop. She noticed how the local towns people, the *Perugini*, would come in on Sunday afternoons after church and ask for chocolates and sweets. So she and her husband opened a small confectionary factory and boutique. When the young Giovanni Buitoni joined the business in 1907, he and Luisa founded Perugina.

He became and remained her business partner, life-long lover, and dear friend.

Their collaboration yielded chocolates and confections still produced exclusively in Umbria, including the creamy gianduia triangle made of chocolate and crushed hazelnuts. In 1914, when the men went off to fight, the women of Umbria took charge in every business sector. Luisa was one of the leaders. She declared that chocolate was essential for the troops, so business prospered. She and Giovanni continued to work together. Many believe that only a couple so in love could have created such delicacies. Perhaps. Luisa and Giovanni were a stellar team. Their collective business acumen and creativity were as unstoppable as their passion for their work, and for each other.

But their signature creation, the one that would give Perugina notoriety and international fame, was one born of necessity. Luisa had wanted to make better use of hazelnut bits that went unused after making *gianduia*, so she ground them, mixed them in with creamy chocolate, rolled the concoction into a ball, put a single hazelnut on top, and dipped it all in harder chocolate. Because of its shape, she first called it a *cazzotto*, a punch, but eventually decided on the name *baci*, meaning kisses. It was sexier. Taglines and advertising copy came easily — *Dammi un bacio. Give me a kiss* could imply the chocolate or the real thing. *Have your first bacio* in Italy would also appeal to the tourists who always associate Italy with romance.

Luisa and Giovanni took it one step further. When you remove the silver and blue foil, there is a filmy paper love note wrapped around the bacio like a hug. It's rumored that Luisa devised the notes to communicate privately with Giovanni, fourteen years her junior. Since their love and friendship, which lasted until her untimely death in 1935, was common knowledge to everyone, even members of her family, this may not be true. However, it's a telling anecdote about an Italian woman and entrepreneur driven by dreams, and the tenacity to do the right thing by the people who worked for her.

Her delectable Baci, she decided eventually, would be housed in a blue box, colors that resembled a star-studded night sky. Her art director, Federico Seneca, created the cover visual, a drawing of a couple in a passionate embrace inspired by the painting Il Bacio in the Pinacoteca di Brera in Milan. This masterwork of Italian Romanticism by Francesco Hayez was considered one of the most visceral representations of a kiss in western art.

Luisa and Seneca played with the lovers' image in advertising, sometimes staging couples of mixed race, at the time considered a scandalous practice. Miuccia Prada displayed the same playful irreverence when the press remarked that her single-dose night cream packets looked like condoms. 'If it's novel it must be Prada,' they wrote. She laughed, adding that the tiny packets were fun to open and almost childlike.

But all those years that I purchased sweaters and skirts from Spagnoli boutiques around the world, I never knew that Luisa was the founder of the Perugina Empire or that she was such a pioneer. Luisa channeled her love of art, humanity, the land, and her work into a voice for social justice and gender equality decades before the rest of us began the conversation. She was probably amused by the reactions of her critics. I picture her shrugging her shoulders as she got on her bike to ride home after a long day's work.

So how did Luisa Spagnoli progress from chocolates to wool? She came up with the idea to raise a special breed of rabbit known for its soft fur on the grounds outside her villa. She then invented a special comb with which to gently comb the hair until it fell off without hurting the animal. In order to go into production, she employed hundreds of women to slowly comb the rabbit hair that yielded the softest, most desirable, most prestigious angora wool found anywhere in the world.

She knew that women would continue to enter the work force, especially after the first world war. Many of these women had infants and small children at home. So she set up both a lactation room and a nursery on the premises. She paid her employees well, provided them with lunch, and made sure they received recognition for their skills and hard work. She was a quintessential leader and mentor. From the soft, ethically sourced rabbit fur, she made the dresses, boleros, blankets, and jackets for which she won national and, eventually, international recognition.

As one of Italy's first and entirely self-made female entrepreneurs, Luisa Spagnoli was a woman of tremendous spirit and vision. She recognized that success was not only about brilliance but also about stewardship. She was a major player in two of Italy's most consequential industries: confectionary and fashion. And for the fans of her stylish garments it was also about purity and sustainability: a connection to and respect for every part of the production chain.

Spagnoli's story takes us back to a time when we wore well-made garments of natural fibers grown in our fields, fabrics cut and sewn by workers who, in most cases, earned a living wage. I am not discounting the rise of sweatshops in factories around the U.S.; my mother worked in one. However, the clothes we wore, especially those from Italy, were treated the way we were taught to treat people: with respect and generosity. We wore them carefully to keep them clean. We washed, ironed, folded, and layered them neatly in drawers or on closet shelves.

In middle school, girls preferred tote bags, so my mother got me one from the leather market in Florence. It was purple and woven like the Bottega Veneta bags seen even then in stores. The stitching was taut and strong. Because we cared for our things and they were neither objects of status nor inexpensive disposables, these objects carried with them a heritage linked to the hands that had created them. The worker was an essential part of the process, as was the source of the raw material. The articles we purchased were part of a complete circle, not unlike that circle of wool strands wrapped around my hands as nonna Laura swiftly rolled the single thread into a ball in front of the fire, Vivaldi or Rossini playing in the background. Years later, I would impress my music teacher with my knowledge of Italian composers. But they were nothing more than a piece of our lives, *intrecciato*, woven into the whole, like the leather of my imitation Bottega Veneta tote.

The whole is that circle of production, from the idea in someone's mind to the land from which the basics are sourced in a humane way, then on to the hands of the farmer, the artisan, the merchant, and finally the beneficiary, who is less a consumer (ideally) and more a carrier of that tradition into the next century. It is an ideal that has gone off course, but I dare say elements of it are coming back.

Luisa Spagnoli's perspective has its acolytes. And in true Italian style, the baton has been passed to many, so I can cite only a few here. Two of the most notable are Brunello Cucinelli, also from Umbria, and Alberta Ferretti, from Le Marche, the region just alongside, bordering the Adriatic. To enter their worlds is to see the extraordinary in action.

TWENTY-ONE

BRUNELLO CUCINELLI: A HUMANISTIC ENTERPRISE

"True Italian craftsmanship is based on treating things with respect and the dignity they deserve, whether it be an apricot or a cashmere sweater."
Brunello Cucinelli, designer

Two years ago while escorting a group on an artisan tour of Florence, I was invited along with my guests to a Brunello Cucinelli event at the JK Place boutique hotel in the Piazza Santa Maria Novella. After a tour of the Basilica and its gardens, our souls infused with the works of Ghirlandaio, Masaccio, and Giotto, our olfactory senses revived by flowers and Tuscan herbs, we were happy to settle in with an Aperol Spritz on an outdoor terrace and take in the silent parade of models in billowy silks and feather-like cashmere.

I spoke with a Florentine seamstress and an expatriate American couple from Boston. They wore the most stylish sneakers I'd ever seen, and as they waved good-bye, they mounted their bicycles and pedaled off toward their new home in San Frediano. Before leaving, the hostess handed me an engraved card inviting me to the Cucinelli boutique for my free gift.

At the boutique the next day I was greeted by Smonetta as if I were a regular customer, my closets replete with their sumptuous cashmere sweaters in supple shades of celadon, cream, and apricot. She guided me to an upholstered chair and held out a velvet tray with the items for gifting: a teal leather change purse, a silver keychain, small and original bracelets to group together. I chose an unusual taupe bracelet, a thick cashmere band embroidered with four rows of silver thread. It tied with four silk and cashmere strands. It was the year's new look, and I loved that it was all about the fabric. Very Cucinelli.

One would expect a world-renowned designer and entrepreneur, presiding over a business of over two million Euros a year, would live in one or several luxurious residences in Milan, New York, or Cannes. He doesn't. Brunello Cucinelli lives with his wife and daughters in Solomeo, a small twelfth-century town in Umbria not far from Perugia or from Castel Riggione, where he was born. He still sleeps in his favorite hilltop bed in their restored renaissance villa.

He goes to work, after a brisk morning swim, at the factory he has built inside a stone castle, and where almost everyone in the town works. This is where he has invested the profits from his clothing line, into the factory and workers, and into renovating and rebuilding his beloved Solomeo.

A passionate reader of Kant, St. Francis, Socrates, Pascal, and Antoine de Saint-Exupéry, Cucinelli operates from an uncompromising vision to build and drive a thriving humanistic enterprise. Respect for the consumer, the worker and the environment infuses every atom of the brand.

As he explains in his book, *A Humanistic Enterprise in the World of Industry*, his business model is inspired by philosophy, ethics and theology. When the 2008 financial crisis hit, he didn't fire a single employee. Instead, he gathered his team together and challenged them to come up with ideas to continue to grow and build the brand. Cucinelli's way is to inspire pride and a sense of community. Everyone lifts up everyone else. Today, the brand has grown from a one-person operation to a company employing over five hundred people, with boutiques in the United States, Europe, and Japan.

Inside his two factories in Solomeo, the old one inside the castle and a more modern factory close by, one hears the persistent hum of knitting machines. People work at the machines or at tables cutting and stitching. They stand beside one another to give direction or to correct the fall of a seam or the finish of a particular detail. Cucinelli pays his employees twenty percent higher than the average, gives them ninety minutes for a delicious Umbrian lunch in the cafeteria, and inspires them to do their very best while enjoying what they do.

"If I give you the right conditions to work, and I put you in a beautiful place, where you feel a little bit better about yourself because you know your work is being used for something greater than producing a profit, maybe you will get more creative, maybe you will want to work more."

He has transformed a renaissance villa into an employee dining hall, restored village buildings, paved new roads, re-designed parks, and built a school and a theater whose façade resembles Rome's Pantheon. In neighboring Castel Riggione, he's constructed a new soccer stadium because he loves the sport both as player and as spectator.

Drawing on the pre-Socratic principle advocated by the philosopher Thales — "a sound mind in a sound body" — he seeks to bring the trifecta of a sound and sustainable community to Solomeo: economic prosperity, intellectual/spiritual growth, and physical well-being. If one element is off, it affects the rest.

TWENTY-TWO

ALBERTA FERRETTI: ROOTED INSPIRATION

"There is no frenzy here and I think that's reflected in my designs."
Alberta Ferretti, designer

Miles from Milano, under a walnut tree on a flowering hillside in Le Marche, Alberta Ferretti sketched her future collections. I imagine she enjoyed the sound of a pencil scrawl and shade across paper, forms taking shape under a furtive hand, and the quiet rhythms of a pastoral region she now called home.

A native of Cattolica, in the neighboring Emilia Romagna, Ferretti came upon Palazzo Viviani in the tiny medieval village Montegridolfo while searching for a second home. At the time, a local painter was selling the thirteenth-century palazzo at auction. It had no roof and was in terrible disrepair, but its bones showed promise, as did its location in the Zen-like Umbrian hills that flow into the Adriatic Sea. From the palazzo's vantage point over valleys and open fields, hidden fortresses, old stone walls, and historic churches sprang into view. What a perfect respite for the traveler who wanted to take her time, and settle into an authentic Italy that feels very much like home, even though home may be thousands of miles away.

As Ferretti perused the grounds, an idea took root. It developed gradually. First, there was the size and structure of the palazzo. As a second home, it was perhaps too grand. However, as a small, artfully designed hotel, it showed promise. She could convert the surrounding buildings into apartments, thereby transforming most of the village into a luxurious, but intimate four-star hotel — an *albergo diffuso*, as the Italians call it—a hotel where rooms are dispersed in various buildings in the village. This makes for an immersive experience as the traveler has to walk through parts of the village to get to a main lobby, meeting local townspeople along the way.

Ferretti felt an unexpected and immediate connection to this unspoiled landscape, as well as to the farmers and fishermen who pressed the local olive oil, made their honey and ricotta according to decades-old traditions, and hauled in the fresh sweet fish of the Adriatic. For the designer, Montegridolfo had a regenerative appeal that the fashionable capitals of Italy could never emulate. Here she could find serenity, traditions preserved, and world-renowned art in authentic and unexpected places. It was a place in which to imagine and to create. And, given the brilliance of her 2016 collection, clearly she made the right professional choice.

Le Marche, not unlike Abruzzo, is barely on tourism's radar, but it deserves to be. The city of Urbino, home of Raffaello, is a UNESCO heritage site. Its discreet neighbor, Ascoli Piceno, is considered one of Italy's most sedate and enchanting cities. The white cliff beaches of the Adriatic and Mt. Sibillino with its wild Parco Nazionale are marvels to explore — experiences to savor without waiting on lines or maneuvering around souvenir kiosks. Le Marche's inconspicuous persona appealed to artisans like Ferretti. It also appealed to a team of investor partners who encouraged her not only to create the hotel but also to restore the entire *borghetto* of Montegridolfo. She needed little encouraging and embraced her dream project with the same imaginative fervor she applies to her collections year after year.

To preserve the basic architecture of Montegridolfo, Ferretti set about to restore all the town's buildings, exterior walls, and the clock tower at the town's center. She made sure to retain the bones and authenticity of the place she had fallen in love with. To step inside Montegridolfo today, even after the restoration, is to immerse oneself in an Italy utterly unspoiled.

As I peruse photographs of the rooms inside the restored Palazzo Viviani, I imagine sleeping in the crisp linens, then opening up my bedroom windows to the scented breezes outside. I look at photos of candlelit dinner tables infused in amber softness and of balconies over green hills. There are gardens and a pool, places I would love to linger in, reclining after a leisurely walk through the renaissance glory that is Urbino. The entire hotel speaks to an understated and inclusive elegance, born of genuineness and simplicity and welcoming to all who venture into it.

We know Italy's art and history are the offspring of its landscape, so it makes sense that one would discover it in refined or raw forms, tucked away inside small churches, secret piazzas, rock formations, and towns one has never heard of. This is where Italian art is most alive, because it's where it has always resided.

Love and respect for our roots and heritage enhance our lives in immeasurable ways. They're the experiences one never forgets. I would not trade for all the five-star resorts in the world those times my brother and I would get out of my zio Peppino's tiny *cinquecento* and run up the hill along the dusty road to nonna Laura's house. I would trade neither that first wobbly and uncomfortable train ride through the tunnels inside the Alps, nor our first sight of the marble hills of Carrara while munching a simple panino from a food vendor cart, nor those early morning raw eggs beat up with sugar and drizzled with Marsala wine, for a private chauffeur and dinner served by a world-renowned star chef.

When I visit Antrosano today, I see the apricot stone house and the vineyards no longer cultivated by nonna Laura's hand, but her energy is still there, affixed to every *grappolo*. I was sad when the family sold it, but as a good friend said, "a house is a place. It becomes special because of the people who are in it."

Cucinelli and Ferretti both know, as did the Plains Indians, that each human life is tethered to the natural world around it, to the earth and to the voices, labor, and handcrafts of those who came before. Through the loss, persistence and renewal of traditions, the space between oceans and generations diminishes. In its place, is a joyful awareness of all we are capable of and all we can create. Armed with such a gift, how can we help but forge extraordinary experiences for ourselves?

TWENTY-THREE

How to Live and Work Italianamente

"Estro is the love for, and active embrace of, spontaneous inspiration that gives unexpected specialness and currency to creative endeavors."
Anton Guadagno, conductor

One afternoon, as I hastily minced parsley and garlic for our annual Christmas Eve dinner, my father took the knife out of my hand. "You have to chop more finely, see?"

"What difference does it make?" I asked, exasperated. I'd had a long workday, we had six more fish to prepare, and I just wanted to get this over with. My father would have none of it.

"It takes just as long to do a job well as it does to do it poorly, so do it right to begin with," he said.

Since I wasn't going to get any sympathy, I set about chopping with the single knife my parents owned, and with which they made the most delicious and memorable food I'd ever eaten in my entire life. Besides, I was not about to argue with my father's Christmas Eve fish dinner mastery. It remains, even years after his passing, my favorite meal of the year.

This mastery was due to three things upon which, for an Italian, there is no compromise: authenticity, simplicity, and the determination to get it right. First came the fish, the freshest available, purchased that same morning at the Arthur Avenue fish market in The Bronx. Unlike most fish markets, where you order from behind a counter, here you get to walk around and in between huge bins of shaved ice and the daily catch, so the fish's eyes stare straight at you. You get to stand by the scale as the fishmonger weighs your selection, and then you set about arguing over how much you're willing to pay. My father checked or chucked each cherrystone and little neck clam. Then he moved on to the *calamaretti* he would scrub down to an impossible shade of whiteness for calamari salad. In the same fashion, we did calamari in stewed tomatoes; eel in oil and vinegar, baked shrimp and filet of sole.

We cleaned the fish ourselves, preparing most of it in varying combinations of the same basic ingredients: olive oil, garlic, parsley, lemon, breadcrumbs, and tomato. That's it. Freshness and simplicity allowed for the precision that naturally followed.

After a few minutes of careful mincing, I forgot about work. Stress fell away as we squeezed and strained lemons, grated breadcrumbs, and sprinkled uniformly cut pieces of garlic and parsley. Even our stuffed clams were bare bones simple, an old family recipe and the very best I've ever had: the juice and meat of the clams, olive oil, bread crumbs, garlic, parsley, and oregano.

We saved the shells to fill with the mixture, and just before we put them in the oven, we drizzled some good olive oil on top. We set the table with mama's holiday linens, real silverware, and vintage glasses from the Canada years. I even found some ripe persimmons, a once yearly staple.

I lit the candles as he turned on the CD player. Bing Crosby sang *"White Christmas."* White headlights lit slits between the venetian blinds. Our family was arriving. In a few minutes they would walk through the front door and place wrapped presents under the tree. We'd hug and kiss, share the Prosecco, and gather around the table. I would have that familiar warm feeling when we were all together, safe in the home where I grew up, black-and-white photos of my grandparents on the mantle. I dimmed the lights and reflected on my father's lesson in mindfulness, given long before becoming a popular and social media-trending term.

When I worked for a Japanese cosmetics company, I found myself at a similar learning crossroads. Just as Clinique's marketing focused relentlessly on language and product positioning, Shiseido's was dogmatic about ritual. There was a precise way to open a bottle of moisturizer, done with a cotton square between two fingers as you removed the top. Then you applied the product on skin in a series of orchestrated strokes, starting in the center of the forehead, left to right and vice versa, around the eyes, and up three strokes on the cheeks and around the chin.

There was an equally precise ritual for using a tissue to remove make up. Instead of crunching the tissue in one's hand and rubbing it any which way, we were to fold it into a triangle, wrap it around a hand as in tea ceremony, and then follow the same movements as we had with the cotton pad. I couldn't see a rationale for this at first, even though it did look clean and graceful, but since I had to learn and teach it, I followed the rituals every morning and night in my own skincare practice. Shiseido used the word practice instead of routine to imply something learned via practice and discipline.

What I gleaned was this. The nightly ritual took no longer than my usual rushed methods. It relaxed me, did a more efficient job, and used less product. In both the Japanese and the Italian vernacular, simple requires thought and concentration. Taking it slow yielded a result at once pragmatic as refined. Consider the precision in origami, in Hoya glass, and in the cut of an Armani jacket.

In his compelling essay "Performing Opera *Italianamente*," written for WQXR, Fred Plotkin, a foremost authority on opera and on all things Italian, recounts his interview with the Sicilian conductor Anton Guadgano. Plotkin has asked Guadagno how he approached opera.

The conductor responds that he works *italianamente* — or, Italian-ly.

Plotkin probes further, although I suspect he already understood where the revered conductor was going. Guadagno's response dispels pervasive and inaccurate stereotypes of the Italian approach to art and to life, including those that portray an undisciplined populace, for whom success is more a matter of charm than pragmatic endeavor.

As Guadagno indicates — and the sheer volume of Italy's achievements in art, architecture, fashion, culinary arts, science, and technology affirm — working *italianamente* yields excellence via three uncompromising principles: "an absolute seriousness about work, a belief in quality in all things (even if achieved with difficulty), and a fatalism about the obstacles life can present." Add to this a fourth principle, and you arrive at an unparalleled practice of art and life: the fundamental Italian belief that anything one creates must meet three criteria—usefulness, durability, and beauty. This combination results in the unmistakable workmanship in Italian shoes and clothing; the skill of Italian carpentry, stone and tile work; the refinement in its cuisine, and balance of flavor in its wines; and the significant achievements in science and education.

Give an Italian woman a project, and she will draw from both sides of the brain, the way a musician balances treble and base notes. She will apply absolute seriousness to the work at hand. There is a reason why a lead soprano is called an *assoluta*. As an artist and as an Italian woman, she gives the absolute best of herself. What happens next is the quality that gives Italian craftsmanship its edge. Guadagno describes it as *estro*.

"*Estro* is the love for, and active embrace of, spontaneous inspiration that gives unexpected specialness and currency to creative endeavors."

We see *estro* within Italy's best conductors when, baton in hand, they summon this inspired love and bring the music to a level even they had not foreseen. Toscanini, Muti, Abbado, Serafin, Guadagno have all been masters of estro.

Estro kicks in, however, only after preparedness has done the hard work. But we all understand it. Have you ever worked on and rehearsed a speech for weeks? And then, miraculously, when you're at the podium, slides clicking behind you, the practiced words start to flow. You speak with an eloquence you hadn't anticipated, and connect with your audience in a way that makes them want to listen. You begin to improvise with unanticipated eloquence. It is in those moments, after tireless preparation to deliver your very best, that the muse arrives and lights the flame.

This is as close as we come to working *italianamente*, when we make the choice to live fully and thus embrace the moment. We experience whatever comes our way with senses, minds, and hearts on high alert. When we scrub off the dictates of status and expectations that tell us how we should live, we allow ourselves to live authentically.

These ingredients for living *italianamente* are the same as those at the root of an Italian woman's style, and her ability to transform the ordinary into extraordinary: heritage, community, and an embedded love of beauty in all its forms.

TWENTY-FOUR

YOUR LIFE IS YOUR BIGGEST WORK OF ART

"The Italians know that everything in their country is imbued with their spirit. They know that there is no need, really, to distinguish or to choose between the smile on the face of a camerière and Donatello's San Giorgio. They are all works of art, the great art of being happy and of making other people happy, an art which embraces and inspires all others in Italy. The only art worth learning, which can never really be mastered."
Luigi Barzini, The Italians

The beauty of a world where travel is encouraged — cultures immigrating, emigrating, and forging new paths — is that we share the best of our cultures and are inspired to re-think and re-shape our lives.

Italy has given the world some of the finest art treasures ever created, not the least of which is *the art of living* — the art Italian women have passed on to successive generations no matter where they were born or where they reside.

Italian women live life as an art form. In true renaissance spirit, they embrace tradition and new ideas. They know that in a predominantly

130

patriarchal world, women are still the driving force that shapes how we live, what we eat and wear, the communities we build, the things we create, and what we leave to successive generations.

The Italian and Italian-American women whose quotes appear on the following pages represent different age groups and generations. Each does her part, in her own way, to preserve her heritage, thereby bringing the extraordinary into her own life and into the lives of others, whether through local family and community efforts, or through the broader channels of entrepreneurship, philanthropy, art, and media.

"When life gives you lemons or ugliness, all you need to do is let your eye travel, look above, and create your own world of beauty."
Francesca Belluomini, fashion savant and author of *The Cheat Sheet of Italian Style*.

"It is only when I am outside Italy that I realize how much I enjoy my Italian traditions. I must have my espresso in the morning, and it has to be good. Bad food is never an option, great shoes are a must, and family is everything."
Flavia Brunetti, author and owner of *Young in Rome*, city blog

"A number of years ago, I took a bike tour of Sicily. I dismounted in an olive grove and sank my hands into the deep warm earth. I began to have a real sense of place. That pile of earth was Sicilian history, generations of olive growing, labor and obstacles. I

started LaRosaWorks to keep that feeling alive."
Karen LaRosa, President of La Rosa Works
Travel

"Italian women distinguish themselves because of our strong traditions and deep roots. American women have always had everything so they consume more and move quickly into the next chapter. Italian women have always had to be frugal so we invest in the long term. We take it slow. Our choices are not always practical or convenient, but they are deeper and more romantic."
Ornella Fado, Television producer of
Brindiamo

"Women well understand the power of reason in shaping our lives for the better, but we also need time for the poetry once cultivated in our grandfathers' gardens and space to measure meaning in the singsong of a child."
Maria Laurino, author of *Old World Daughter.*
New World Mother

"The Italian and Italian-American women I have known and loved share the same characteristics of being strong, confident, determined, yet gentle and feminine."
Dr. Marie-Elena Liotta, linguist, educator,
Chairperson and Trustee of the Enrico Fermi
Scholarship Foundation

Those qualities, determination, and imagination, infused with a passion to look for and create beauty, make Italian women resilient and resourceful. In fashion design and entrepreneurship, after Elsa Schiaparelli and Simonetta Colonna di Cesarò, we had Mariuccia Mandelli, who took a small artisan business in Milan with just a handful of workers and built a knitwear empire in a very short time. Her secret? She was *sfacciata* — the Italian word for brazen. She brought her designs to the most prestigious fashion events in Florence (the Pitti show) and Milan, before anyone in the industry even knew her name. As far as she was concerned, her anonymity at the time was a minor hurdle.

When Ottavio and Rosita Missoni established their business partnership, they drew upon Ottavio's unique understanding of sportswear (he participated in the London Olympics) and Rosita's family background in the clothing business. Their collaboration in both design and production have given us the stunning, sometimes zany color palettes and graphic patterns of Missoni knitwear, coveted around the world. Who doesn't dream in Missoni every now and then? I still remember my friend Luisa Cacciatore in a knit coat of russet, red, blue and gold. Today she might wear a re-imagined Missoni, designed by Rosita's equally talented daughter, Angela.

After Salvatore Ferragamo returned to Italy from a successful career in Hollywood, he opened a small family business in Palazzo Spini Feroni in Florence. He married Wanda in 1940 and they had six children. In 1960, Salvatore died and Wanda took over the business. Under her stewardship, the Ferragamo brand became an industry leader in footwear and leather goods and branched further into perfumes, clothing, and exquisite hotel properties — the Lungarno in Florence and Castiglion del Bosco near Montalcino. Even though the company bears only her husband's name, it was Wanda Ferragamo who drove the family business to new heights.

Female succession and management of Italian family-owned

companies is not unusual. When Mario Prada, a renowned leather craftsman who was the first to showcase his luxury leather goods and bags inside Milano's Galleria, died in 1958, his daughter Luisa took control of the business. Just twenty years later, the baton passed to Luisa's daughter Miuccia, and the rest is history: innovative clothing and accessories in unexpected materials, the iconic Prada backpack made of nylon, the understated labeling, collections which subverted preconceived notions of beauty and luxury, the diffusion line Miu Miu, and the arrival of the young female entrepreneur.

Donatella Versace took over the Versace brand under different and more difficult circumstances. Her brother's murder catapulted her into the forefront of efforts to preserve a brand so firmly associated with Gianni Versace the persona, no one could imagine it without him. Donatella, in spite of her grief and the doubts circulating around the media sphere, was determined to triumph. And she has, on her own terms, creating a unique design aesthetic that celebrates renewal and the transformative power of the self.

TWENTY-FIVE

ITALIAN WOMEN CELEBRATE FEMININITY

"Italians think women are fantastic, and they design to make them even more fantastic."
Elizabeth Hurley, model

O n a breezy autumn morning, I meet my friends Alessandra and Angela at a café along Via delle Belle Donne (Road of Beautiful Women) in Florence. We remove our sunglasses, swivel heads for the cheek to cheek kiss, and exclaim, *"Che bella giornata!"* All along the street, the artisans open up their shops, the scent of espresso wafts through the air, woven with the smell of lilacs tossed inside the iron gates of a florist's shop. I'm in Italy, and I allow time to take me along its assigned travels according to the Italian saying: *Chi va piano va sano e lontano, (She who goes slowly travels well and far.)*

Alessandra, an art historian and a native Florentine, is quietly elegant in a soft peach, belted trench, and a voluminous scarf from Manila Grace on Via dei Pescioni. She loves to balance the classics with something unexpected. Grounded and deeply intellectual, she has the grace and gravitas to make the spontaneity work. I smell her familiar fragrance, the one she's worn since she was a teenager, and I tear up. It's been so many months, and it's just now that I realize how much I've missed her.

Angela, meanwhile, has just returned from her wedding and

honeymoon in Mexico. She is Mexican by birth. She fell in love with Florence and with a young Italian architect during a vacation and decided to move here. They were married shortly afterwards. Angela opened a business as a personal shopper who shows visitors how to bring Italian style into their lives. She hands me a small gift bag and inside is a 25 ml flacon of Bulgari's *Jasmine Noir*. It sits in the palm of my hand like an eighteenth-century amulet, its shape reminiscent of cabochon stones from the Bulgari jewelry collection. I twist off the gold cap and I am in love.

If Alessandra's style is contemporary classic, Angela's is sexier and more whimsical. Alessandra prefers to navigate the cobblestone streets through her neighborhood of San Frediano in ballerina flats or Tod's style loafers, in a compelling color. Angela can stride up and down Via Tornabuoni in her snakeskin stilettos with greater ease and quickness than intrepid New Yorkers rushing to work in commuter sneakers. Alessandra is lanky and fair, Angela is curvy and olive skinned.

Both women are comfortable in their own skin. They are at one with their body image and their fashion choices. They don't stress about weight, clothes, food, or what others think. If they stop at Vestri in Santa Croce for a gelato or an artisanal chocolate, they don't concern themselves with calories. They will talk about how good the chocolate is and how it's made from genuine cacao grown on the owner's plantation in South America, or how the gelato uses the world's finest pistachios. These pistachios are from Sicily, of course.

Our espresso arrives with a cornetto wrapped in a paper napkin on our plates. A *spremuta d'arancio*, pressed before our eyes from Sicilian blood oranges, is poured into glass goblets. I'm once more at Caffè Canova in Rome on the day my mother, wrapped in her sweeping white coat, enchanted a man ten years her junior. Forty years have passed, and the ritual and presentation are the same: espresso and *spremuta* in ceramic and crystal, the *cornetto* baked that morning. As modern as Florence has become with its trendy shops and fashionista vibe, it still holds onto the refined traditions that bring people together. We talk about clothes and how for women in Italy they are a source of joy, not a source of stress. Italian women don't open the door to a jammed closet in the morning or before an important event and exclaim they have nothing to wear. In the spirit of *Compra Meno, Compra Meglio,* they don't over purchase. Whatever hangs in their closets or sits folded inside a cedar-scented armoire is loved, cared for, and worn over and over again with different accessories and in imaginative ways. They mix old and new, and high and low. This adds to the fun. When you have less, what you own is precious. You respect and preserve it. When you clear away the clutter imposed by others, life opens up and gives you permission to play.

In Rome, I see this precious playfulness in a black-and-white evening pantsuit paired up with a sexy silk camisole and black Converse sneakers with a wedge heel. It works because the proportions are right, and the woman wearing it does so without apology and with a wicked sense of humor. She doesn't care whether we approve of her fashion choice. There is something delightfully irreverent in the Italian psyche that says, *Want to judge me? Go for it. Want to compete with me? Knock yourself out.*

It's not about the label. It's about the art. Consider the espresso the barista has just placed on the bar. We know that for him, even this simple task is art. It only appears effortless because he has worked *italianamente* to learn it. In the words of Jean Cocteau, "Style is a simple way of saying complicated things." As in the Japanese tea ceremony or at the dinner table in a French home where children are taught to uncork a wine bottle, show its label to a guest, and pour the wine correctly, the ritual of preparing and serving espresso is a reflection of Italian history and a source of national pride. I admit that not even in New York City, or really anywhere else in the world, do baristas make espresso with such effortless grace as they do here in Italy.

Later that day when we stop for lunch, Angela and Alessandra channel Luisa Cacciatore. We have a craving for the *paccheri* with seafood, accompanied by a glass of organic wine from the winery *Ama*. We chatter about the freshness of the seafood and how the sweet cherry tomatoes enhance the flavor of pasta that is just firm enough. We don't rush because it is rare the three of us see each other, so we want to hold onto these moments.

By doing so, we build on our own sense of community or mini-communities. Whenever I'm in Italy for work or holiday, whether looking at art in the Brancacci Chapel, selecting dress fabrics in La Casa dei Tessuti, or taking long walks to discover hidden piazzettas in unexplored neighborhoods, I meet up regularly with friends. I make new acquaintances inside museums, bars, and cafés. We exchange phone numbers and email addresses. We visit each other in our respective cities. The circle of friendships expands, not unlike the circular walls around Florence that expanded with each succeeding century. We set a time to come together to drink an aperitivo and rest our feet, which quite often are now cradled inside a pair of beautiful Italian shoes.

For the Italian-American woman, it's a gift our heritage has passed on to us. It dares us to feel guilty about that hazelnut truffle, or that new pair of red stilettos that updates a vintage dress. Because no matter how many generations removed, the date on your passport, or the state of your finances, that unmistakable Italian *je ne sais quoi* is part of our DNA, and we will work it however we wish.

TWENTY-SIX

EFFORTLESS CHIC

"There is an appearance of effortlessness in the way that Italians can dress."
Emilia Fox, actress

Sprezzatura is the Italian art of looking good without trying too hard. For the Italian woman, getting dressed is yet one more of life's pleasures, a seamless extension of her way of life, a chance to get creative with color and form, to take it slow, to curate with intelligence and poetry, and to throw in a dash of playfulness that is uniquely hers.

How does she do it and how can you incorporate Italian style into your day to day? The process is both philosophical and tactile. It engages the artistic and romantic parts of you. Add a sense of humor, be bold, don't take yourself too seriously, and don't be afraid to shake things up.

Italian Women Don't Put Off Happiness.

No matter how busy we are, we make time for family, friends and for small pleasures throughout the day. We figure out ways to shoehorn everything in. We don't want to miss anything or anyone. It's our sense of fatalism. Each day can be our last day on earth, so let's find joy wherever we can and celebrate what we have.

139

We see beauty wherever it appears.

Please forgive us if we're so easily distracted. If, while we're walking down a New York street together in early spring and we're deep in conversation, and without provocation we notice the arching branches of pink and white blossoms, and we stop to comment, take photos, or dance in the street, do not take offense. We do this. No matter how frantic the day, and with much love for whomever we are with, we simply cannot let beauty pass us by unnoticed.

We know that joy doesn't come from the big stuff.

We save up for vacations and objects, but true joy is felt in the simple moments we sprinkle into our daily lives: a hug from a friend, a piece of chocolate, an espresso while looking out the window at the rain, a walk in the rain, a chance encounter, smelling a tomato from our garden and making a simple sauce with it, or holding a door open for someone who needed that kind gesture at just that moment.

We make time to sit down for a good meal.

No matter how small the meal, we don't eat in a hurry or while walking in the street. The extraordinary is about being fully in the moment. We prefer real plates to paper or plastic. The ritual, even abbreviated, is as important as the meal itself. When I worked for a Prada skincare start-up, we put in twelve-hour days. But at lunchtime, we all stopped, went into the small kitchen, and put our lunch on plates. We took time to eat, and finished up with an espresso. We still got our work done.

We stop for magic.

Several days ago, as I crossed Central Park just outside the Metropolitan Museum of Art, I heard a violinist playing. Around me, the spring flowers were in bloom, children played on the statue of Alice in Wonderland. Swiftly I redirected my path to follow the music. I finally saw him playing under one of those marvelous stone archways that just sneak up on you when you're daydreaming. People stopped to listen and to throw coins into a basket. I noticed a small boy stare at the musician, fascinated. The woman walking with him took his hand and told him they had to hurry. He followed but kept looking back at the wooden instrument in the man's hand. He had never seen a violin before and was probably wondering how it could make such a beautiful sound. I have no doubt they either had a plane to catch or an appointment to get to. But if they didn't, what a shame. In our world today, we are always in a hurry and we miss the poetry around us. The Italian knows to stop and listen to it.

I remember one morning in the Estée Lauder offices, I was holding a meeting when a message interrupted us: My father had stopped in to see me. I was mortified. Was he dressed the right way? What kind of an impression would he make? He came in with a tray of cups of espresso for all the women at my meeting. They thought he was adorable, that he looked like Antonioni. After a short break, very good espresso, and good conversation, he blew kisses good-bye and we got back to work. Not surprisingly, we were more inspired and productive than before. When the magic is there, grab it.

Bad food is never an option.
Including and especially after a hard workday. Chopping up a fresh tomato, garnishing a slice of mozzarella with basil, grilling a piece of fish with lemon, or pulling together an impromptu plate of spaghetti *aglio e olio* and placing real plates on the table — these do more to relax and connect us than does opening plastic containers of prepared foods made with ingredients we don't know or can't pronounce.

We take our espresso very seriously.
A subject on which there is no compromise. It has to be good. It has to be the real thing. And it tastes best in Italy. Each time as the plane descends over Fiumicino, all I can think about is my very first espresso in Rome. From then on it's that tiny delectable treat several times a day. For Italians espresso is an artisanal jewel and a matter of national pride. Don't even think of watering it down for that atrocity called an Americano or mixing it up with carmel syrup or pumpkin

spice. Would you mix ginger ale in a glass of *Brunello* or *Sant'Emilion?*

Caffè culture in Italy is simple. Cappuccino or *caffè latte* in the morning before noon; espresso at any time of day. You may do an *espresso macchiato* (espresso with a dash of foamed milk) or a *marocchino* (same as the macchiato but with a dash of chocolate). That's it. If you ask for a latte you will get a glass of milk and the barista will give you an odd look. Italians don't drink glasses of milk, we don't drink cappuccino after an afternoon or evening meal, and we don't do flavoring in coffee, ever.

The presentation is always the same, whether in a bar in Milan or in a tiny hillside town no one has ever heard of — it is serious and elegant, romantic and literary. An art, distilled exquisitely into a small ceramic cup.

We trust our instincts.

If you have a craving for fruit, gelato, pastry, cheese, have it. There is a reason your body and your spirit make this request. It is either a nutritional need or a spiritual one. The important thing is not to overdo. Small amounts savored slowly. A single dark chocolate truffle or a scoop of truly artisanal gelato will satisfy your cravings and you won't indulge too much.

We eat better food, so we eat less.

That is why travelers to Italy marvel at how little weight they gain there, even while enjoying morning pastries, noontime pastas, glasses of wine, *bistecca Fiorentina*, and evening aperitivi.

We rarely snack.

But we always have fresh or self-prepared food on hand just in case: fruit, nuts, stewed lentils, quinoa, greens to toss for a salad, Italian tuna, dried chickpeas, fava, and cannellini beans. My lifetime favorite is a tiny dish of first-press olive oil and a chunk of bread. I literally crave it in the middle of the day, another reason Italian women have such glowing skin.

Chapter Twenty-Six

We follow our senses.

The intoxicating scent of peonies and lilacs in spring. The taste of a fresh tomato from our garden. A bluer spring or a summer sky. It wakes us up to color. This is when my dark winter wardrobe palette recedes. I reach for the pinks, the corals, the lilacs, the luminous whites.

Let nature's seasons guide your style choices. Pull out what you already own or find that single artisanal accessory that makes you smile; let it be your fashion signature this season. Throw it over the outfits you usually wear so you don't wear them the same way. Wear pearls with your jeans and casual shirts, a snug leather jacket with dresses, and silver Superga sneakers with trouser suits. Add an unexpected accent, maybe an antique brooch from a local flea market that says, *I'm alive and I'm loving it.*

During my last trip to Florence, I purchased a string of glass beads; some are white, others are clear, some are marbleized or striped in the same white and clear motif. I love its freshness and its weight. It's fun and whimsical, but it can be classic if I want it to be. And it looks great with summer white.

In the Istanbul bazaar, I found a silver and white bracelet and it cost all of two dollars, but I always get compliments on it, and every time I wear it I think of the smell of couscous and kebab, tiny cups of apple tea. I see the Turkish rugs in burnished reds, golds, and cool celadon, and I feel the misting water machine overhead that kept us cool in the sweltering August heat.

While in an outdoor market in Positano one summer, Steve spotted a linen sheath dress in a gorgeous shade of blue. It's rare these days, with clothing mass produced so quickly, to find truly beautiful and unique colors. But this color made my heart sing. The dress was a deep warm blue, the color of the Mediterranean sky, embellished with just a handful of tiny pearls at the neck. A small tulle ruffle ran along the asymmetrical hem. It's a dress that says with impassioned delight: *summer* and *limoncello.*

I so miss the diversity of color before fast-fashion times. When greens, rich russets, and mustard yellows ushered in a rejuvenating fall and the cuddly sweater season. The luminous whites and creams of summer. The dancing florals of spring. I have a nostalgic affection for the era when warm whites and bordeaux heralded the snowy winter when all you want is a cognac and a good book. Not only do our immense, speedy, and centralized systems for delivering food and clothing wreak havoc with our planet, they deprive us of the sensory joy of feeling alive and in the moment. A growing number of artisans seek out that sensory joy once more, starting new slow initiatives in food and fashion, and today's millennials are leading the charge.

We buy less, buy better, and use what we have.

I rarely purchase anything new for a special event. I first check out what I already own. When we make the conscious choice to work with what we have, we're surprised by our own creativity. We bring joy into the process, rather than add the stress of shopping, accompanied by buyer's remorse after spending money for something we don't need, often to impress people we don't know. To draw a romantic metaphor, the immediate gratification purchase is the one night-stand; the other is an intimate and somewhat complicated partner who, even after many years, still enchants you in bed.

We love to play dress-up.

I recently had to put together an outfit for a black-and-white Gatsby night. I don't own a flapper dress, so chose my 1940s black-and-white polka-dot dress, and dug out a vintage pair of Ferragamo spectator pumps. The black-and-white shoes are over thirty years old and are still beautiful. What's more, because Ferragamo makes a longer last, they were so comfortable, I not only could stand in them all night, I could dance in them, too.

Similarly, when I needed Indian attire for a Bollywood dance party, I used a pink Thai silk tunic trimmed in silver that my mother had made for me over forty years ago. Back then, I wore it as a dress. Yes, it's Thai and not Indian, but the colors and the motif worked. I found a flowing scarf at a market in Flushing, Queens. Matched up white pants, silver sandals, it needed just long earrings and some bangles from a local flea market. I was set to dance. I also now had yet another summer look: the tunic with slim white pants and silver sandals — something that is exclusively me.

We have a keen sense of place.

There are outfits I put together to suit certain settings. If I'm going to a Greek restaurant, I will wear something blue and white; if for tapas and sangria, then coral earrings or a shawl that reminds me of Spain. I have a pale green linen sundress from Ravello. It was relatively inexpensive, but I loved the subtle tie-dyed effect and transparent lace patterns. A bit Jerry Garcia and Monica Vitti. It makes me feel sexy and feminine on a hot day. It breathes and flows when I walk, and I've never seen anything remotely like it.

A theater evening calls to mind a trouser suit, perhaps with a white shirt and a bow at the neck, or a flowing dress with velvet pumps— even a pair of jeans paired up with a Chanel-style jacket and fake pearls.

We summon our inner diva whenever we feel like it, just because...

Yes, every Italian woman, regardless of generation, has an element of badass. Look as far back as Elsa Schiaparelli and Luisa Spagnoli or at the writings of Franca Sozzani and the inimitable Oriana Fallaci. We know to embrace tradition and shrug off convention. The same woman who spends a Saturday in jeans and an apron, rolling out a paper-thin sfoglia for tagliatelle with an old-fashioned broomstick inherited from her grandmother, may don a Prada slip dress in the evening, perhaps with a pair of vintage platforms and a single piece of jewelry from an aunt or a beloved friend who is no longer there, but who still lives inside the heart. She will listen to a Chopin sonata one minute and Rihanna the next. She's as enchanted by Bollywood as she is by Fellini. She will simply not accept the status quo. She knows it's destined to change, as it well should.

TWENTY-SEVEN

SHE WHO SPENDS MORE, SPENDS LESS.

"Less is More"
Ludwig Mies van der Rohe, architect

A few years ago, without checking my closet first while preparing for a business trip to Monte Carlo, I decided that I needed a number of new pieces. In an immediate gratification frenzy, I bought several pairs of pants, some tunic tops, and tee shirts, and I racked up over three hundred dollars in purchases.

I hung these alongside my older pieces on the closet rack used for planning my travel wardrobe. Generally, I decide on a color palette around which all the pieces work, and I carefully go through the lined-up garments to assess their strengths, discarding as I go along. The new clothes, tags still on them, kept getting pushed farther and farther back. I'd pulled out my all-time travel favorites, those that roll up in a neat little ball and weigh nothing in my suitcase, some of my sartorial go-tos, which I've owned for years, as well as whimsical pieces or accessories with stories connected to them. My one caveat is that everything pack easily and multi-task.

A day later, I returned all the new clothes I'd purchased. For that same trip, however, I needed something elegant for the final night — a gala in the Hôtel de Paris in Monte Carlo. I wanted something simple, unique, and packable. It also had to be a piece I would wear again.

Luckily, I had saved two gift cards for Saks Fifth Avenue and they were having a 75% off sale. For weeks, I'd been stalking a long, black Issey Miyake Pleats Please dress. I bought it for a fraction of the original price, using the monies I'd saved returning the other pieces. I will wear this dress over and over again for the next twenty years in different ways, because Miyake can easily be formal or informal, its beauty timeless.

Now I needed a shawl. After perusing shops for overpriced low-quality sweaters and wraps, I went back into my trusted closet — thank you Francesca Belluomini for your fabulous blog, *Trusted Clothes*. I know my closet loves me. It really does.

I dug out a short black quilted Anne Fontaine jacket that I hadn't worn in years but saved because of its quality. I matched up a cheap pearl and rhinestone choker from a notions shop. It was all easy to pack and a joy to wear. Meanwhile, the dress could go casual on another day with a flat gladiator sandal and no jewelry.

For maximum fun when putting together a travel wardrobe, think of chameleon-like pieces like these. Take stock of what you own. Touch it, try it on. Decide what you will keep. Hang it up in a place where you'll see it. Match it up with unlikely pieces in your wardrobe. Wear it. Don't wait for those "special occasions" in life. Every day is a special occasion.

Items I've splurged on over the years, and I'm glad I did.

White Burberry's trench coat: It reminds me of Audrey Hepburn in *Breakfast at Tiffany's*.

YSL trouser suit: Purchased when the designer was still alive. No one will ever design a trouser suit the way he did. I wear it with a pair of lace-up platforms or just wear the jacket with faded jeans. The gathered waist trousers, many say, are out of style, but they pair well with a black silk blouse and pumps. My only regret is that I didn't buy its style twin: the venerable *smoking*.

Black linen YSL sheath with red belt: Purchased in the 1980s on Rue du Faubourg Saint-Honoré in Paris when the dollar was king.

Every sweater my mother has knitted for me.

Tiffany silver hoops: They gleam like nothing else.

Anne Fontaine white shirts: I hand wash and re-wear them often.

Wolford opaque black hose: I've owned the same four pairs for over ten years. They fit beautifully, have a soft elegant sheen, never run, and I don't have a drawer full of stockings with pulls and snags.

Issey Miyake long black dress: Enough said earlier, but a great, easily packable black dress is always a win.

A 40s-style black and white polka-dot dress by a German designer I never heard of: It's gorgeous. Wrap it, roll it. It will forever be my go-to, and I will wear it over and over again.

An orange and white polka-dot (anything with dots) shirtwaist dress in 50s-style polished cotton.

Black cashmere turtlenecks, good jeans, ankle boots.

A white Max Mara alpaca coat.

My mother's black ottoman coat made in the 1940s.

Manila Grace pieces: Purchased in Florence. I buy one piece each time I visit. I like their commitment to sustainability and local production.

Han Feng pleated scarf: I'm a sucker for her and Issey Miyake's pleats.

Well-cut blazers from Prada, Benetton, J. Crew — or any well-cut blazer, for that matter. For business presentations, nothing says power better. While shopping in Rome with my cousin Alba, an attorney, I noticed that with each dress she purchased a matching jacket for cold evenings or to give the dress a professional polish. A blazer, remember, is your best friend in summer to slip on over a dress at the office for an impromptu meeting or to fend off the effects of air conditioning. Although business casual is the norm in most offices today, there is much truth to the statement by Joi Gordon, CEO of Dress for Success, "When you dress up, you think up."

Italians always like to take it up a notch. Effortless chic is comfortable but curated.

Prada skirts: Purchased with my employee discount or at the Prada outlet outside Florence. Prada does the coolest things with skirts.

A wild boho-style Krizia skirt in orange, lavender, burgundy, celadon: It's like a box of crayons.

Ballerina flats and ankle boots by Stuart Weitzman.

Good Italian shoes: With style and heels I can still walk in, although not for hours on New York City streets. That's why packable ballerinas accompany me everywhere.

An Elsa Peretti cuff bracelet: Not my splurge, but a surprise gift from Steve. It's like wearing a piece of sculpture.

A plain hammered silver ring I purchased from an artigiano in Florence.

What I gladly donate when I'm purging.

Anything that speaks to what I ought to be versus who I am.

Anything that's lost its magic.

Anything that feels or looks dated.

Biggest mistakes.

Clothes that don't fit well, especially at the armholes. Bad fit is the enemy of style.

And buying what I don't need because the price was good.

If you total all the too good to pass up purchases you've made in a month, I bet you could have afforded that one special pair of shoes; had some additional funds for a good vacation; or could have augmented your 401K.

Biggest opportunities.

Know the designers and styles you love. Find out when their sales are and save up. I know when one of my shoe stores has its twice-a-year 40% off sale. I save up and buy one pair, instead of two pairs of a lower-quality shoe.

Check out sample sales. That's where you get some of the best prices. Tell yourself you will walk away with one truly unique item you will love wearing.

Your closet: Chances are you have cool accessories stashed away or a garment that can be re-purposed.

Know the proportions that look best on you and gravitate to those. Tailoring is key.

Re-invent and re-purpose.

I love the process of switching out spring and summer clothes for fall and winter. It's when I make my best discoveries.

Twice a year go through this exercise. Lay out all your seasonal clothes. Set aside donations. Look for places that will actually re-cycle the clothing you donate.

Now look to see what you can put together in interesting ways. Take your time. Play music. Move the pieces around like a chessboard. Have belts, jewelry and scarves handy. If something makes you curious—like a fabric you adore—go with it. It's your sense of style waking up.

Some possibilities.

Remember those gathered waist trousers they told us went out of date? Pair them up with a soft pussy-bow blouse and edgy ankle boots and you're Katherine Hepburn, but with twenty-first-century twist. You may decide to curl your hair that evening or wear a darker lipstick. Go out and order a martini.

I recently pulled out a silk skirt by the Italian designer Pancaldi, known for his light and sumptuous silks. I hadn't worn it in years but had kept it because the colors — gold, peach, lavender, russet — remind me of faded majolica tiles in Italy. Over it, I placed a belted coral jacket from my Prada years. Wow! I have the perfect shoes for it too. Gold gladiators.

Your grandmother's black taffeta evening dress with the sweetheart collar is your in-house vintage find. Match up a pair of red sandals or fun platforms to make it new again.

A dress that's too short could be the cutest tunic over leggings with boots, or layered over a flowing chiffon skirt with lace-up ballerina flats. I also like the look of a dress over leggings and flats to change things up.

An antique broach or cameo can be affixed to a ribbon worn around the neck as a choker.

I love vintage jewelry pieces. They connect me to the stories of people I know, have known, or have never met. I still own a filigreed and jade broach in the shape of a fan given to me by an actress I met by chance in Paris over twenty years ago. I was walking down the stairs in the apartment I'd rented in Montparnasse and saw an open door. I heard an elderly woman's voice call out and entered. To this day I remember that the room smelled of lilacs and patchouli. She was sitting up in her grand bed with a cup of jasmine tea. She told me she'd performed at the Odéon, had met Maria Callas in New York, and that I should try the pastis at Brasserie Lipp. Whenever I'm in Paris I have a pastis in honor of Marie-Sophie. I will always stop by the Odéon. And I think of her often in spring when I cross Lilac Walk in Central Park.

Most important: Find a local seamstress. Lavish her with praise and adoration. She is your talisman of happiness in the style world. Trust her eye above all else. I speak from experience.

Packing chic.

Look for lightweight items that can multi-task and roll up into a ball.

Weeks before you start packing, decide on a basic color palette: three colors that work and play well together so you can change things up at whim. Don't forget that single fabulous scarf or necklace that can add pizzazz without a second thought.

Make a day-to-day list of outfits. Once you have your palette it's easy to switch things around and get creative when your plans change.

Next to each outfit on the page, list the shoes, stockings, and accessories you will wear it with in a separate column. When you're done, you will have a complete storyboard of what you will need, what you can eliminate, and which accessories can multi-task across outfits. And you are less likely to forget something.

You want to pack in a way that gives you more, not less freedom, and the ability to change things up at a moment's notice.

Shoes — the hardest part for me.

Think both style and comfort and always have packable ballerinas handy.

I generally board the plane in my heaviest pair of shoes so as not to have to carry them. Stylish slip-ons or ankle boots with a thick sole make it easier to go through security, run through airports and train stations, and look good as I'm checking into my hotel in Rome.

With all the attractive *calzature* options today, women no longer have to choose between style and comfort. I also bring one or two pairs of dress shoes and my workout shoes.

Handbags.

Thanks to Miuccia Prada it is now acceptable to travel with a nylon backpack or handbag or even a lightweight tote. Consider a cross body nylon bag for the flight and for sightseeing, freeing your hands to take photos. Pack a chic clutch bag for evenings out and a foldable tote to carry shoes, paperwork, and small purchases. It can also double as an overnight or weekend bag should you meet someone interesting in the dining car on that train ride between Zurich and Milan.

Accessories.

I never travel with expensive jewelry other than my wedding band, a silver Elsa Peretti pendant, and a pair of small diamond studs, which my husband gave me for our wedding anniversary. Since these never leave my person, they are safe. I then pack some fun earrings, two necklaces to change up a daytime outfit, several small bracelets, and two or three scarves. Each accessory has its own story. I always bring a pashmina in my carry-on, which holds only four other items: passport, IPad, in flight toiletries case, and writer's notebook.

Toiletries.

Instead of large bottles and jars, opt for several small recyclable containers. That way you can discard as you go along, and your bag gets lighter.

Remember you can always purchase what you run out of in charming perfumeries and apothecaries wherever you are in the world. And it's a chance to discover new products in a different retail environment. You can find exceptional skincare products in pharmacies for example.

Whether packing or purchasing, the Mies van der Rohe principle applies here as well. Less is more.

While I say no rules....

There are just some things you will never see an Italian girl do....

Wear tee shirts with writing on them—unless you're talking the white tee shirt stylishly emblazoned with *We should all be feminists* in black and white, a quote from Chimamanda Ngozi Adichie and sent down the runway by Maria Grazia Chiuri, the first female artistic director for Dior. In a photo she wears it under an impeccable black blazer. A great look that can work with a skirt, jeans, or white pants rolled up at the cuff and teamed up with silver Supergas or even classic ballerinas.

Wear workout clothes when we're not working out. We don't do sweatpants, sweatshirts, and running sneakers as daywear.

Wear cheap shoes. Cheap shoes are never a win. The word cheap doesn't exist in the Italian vocabulary. We may say that in a particular boutique *si compra bene* (one can buy well/at a good price), but cheap implies inferior quality and fast fashion that ends up in landfills. Remember my mother's adage: Good shoes can make an inexpensive dress look like couture, and the opposite is equally true. While on the subject, rubber flip flops are for pedicures and pools. Period.

Wear something too tight, too sexy, too suggestive. Trying too hard for effect is anathema to Italian style.

Wear unsightly beat up sneakers or running shoes while traveling or touring. It says tourist right away. With so many options today there are no excuses. Italians do wear sneakers but always well cared for and stylish ones, whether a Converse type canvas pair or thicker lace-ups in brushed suede, Geox style. In loafers or boots with good soles, one can walk for hours. Trust me, we New Yorkers walk everywhere and all day long—without sacrificing style.

If you're walking around Rome, even on cobbled streets, you will eventually end up at a wine bar surrounded by exquisitely dressed Italians in casual wear that is no less comfortable but infinitely chicer. You will wonder how they pulled themselves together in such an insouciant way. You will see them smiling, feeling good in their skin, happy with their choices, not because of what their clothing costs but because of the fun they had putting it together. With just a few good pieces you can do the same.

Style Guides and Guidance

There comes a time when we seek out the experts. Style guides abound but there are those I consider a head above the best. They are my perennial go-tos because, like a good espresso, they are en pointe — strong, good, and provocative.

For quintessential Italian style, the bible is Francesca Belluomini's *The Cheat Sheet of Italian Style: Sustainable Chic in Ten Struts.*

I also recommend Parisian Chic: *A Style Guide by Ines de la Fressange* and,

How To Get Dressed — A Costume Designer's Secrets for Making Your Clothes Look, Fit, and Feel Amazing by Alison Freer.

Daily skincare is essential.

We can sum it up in the words of Coco Chanel:

"Nature gives you the face you have at twenty; it is up to you to merit the face you have at fifty."

I have a built-in bias on this subject. My mother has beautiful skin because she never sunbathed and because she has always used lavish night creams and day creams. Skincare and cosmetics have been a part of my life for decades, and I confess I still enjoy swirling up lipstick tubes of the newest colors, spraying scent strips with the latest Jo Malone scent, and trying out samples of the newest facial oils.

In skincare today there are so many choices and price points women are free to choose what works for them, be it simple or more complicated, and the emergence of sustainable, eco-friendly, and cruelty-free brands yields an entire new arena to explore.

But the basics are non-negotiable: cleanser, daily moisturizer, sun block, and eye cream. Never sleep with make up on. Exfoliate once a week, or however often your skin requires, to remove dead skin cells. A weekly masque will also keep your skin toned and healthy.

I love serums and nightly facial oils because they absorb so well and make the skin silky soft. But if creams and lightweight lotions are better for the overall health of your skin, go with it.

All this care however, is for naught if skin is not hydrated and nourished from the inside. The basics come into play here; nutritional meals rich in fruits, vegetables, and Omega 3 fatty acids; lots of water; exercise. Avoid or cut back on sugar, especially from processed foods; this will reduce the inflammation that accelerates skin aging.

Finally, fall in love, make love, take a long walk through a garden, make your life extraordinary in little ways every day, and your skin will have that glow that will make people wonder....What is she up to?

Perfume.

My friends in Florence love to tell the story of how Catherine de Medici brought fashion, cuisine, and perfumery to France. As the new queen, she did not bring a generous dowry. What she did bring was style, good taste, and the *go beyond convention* verve that courses through the veins of every Tuscan.

According to legend, Catherine arrived in France with her personal perfumer, Rene de Florentin, and shortly afterwards introduced perfumed gloves to the French court. The gloves were scented to mask the unpleasant odor of the leather, using compositions of herbs, spices, woods, and flowers, including jasmine, violet, rose, and orange blossoms. The perfume industry was born.

Whether considered alchemy, aphrodisiac, fashion staple, or aromatherapy, perfume is one of life's most visceral pleasures. It's the last thing I apply before I walk out in the mornings and at night before I go to bed.

I received my first bottle of Diorissimo from my father on Christmas Eve when I was just fifteen. I remember the soft pink and gray Dior colors on the box, the designer's favorite color combination inspired by his native home in Normandy. The first whiff revealed the most stylized lily of the valley top note in fragrance history. Outside snow was falling but Diorissimo was the promise of spring, of an incipient coming of age romance, and perhaps a first kiss on a bridge in Venice under winter fog. Lily of the valley was Dior's magical good luck talisman. No Dior gown ever swept the catwalk without a sprig of the tiny bell-shaped flower tucked inside it. It is the one mono-floral perfume that has survived the test of time, a scent so memorable that even today I'm able detect the changes in formulation. I know, without question, that if a perfumer were to re-create the original magical Diorissimo, it would bring into sharp relief all the memories of that Christmas and the months leading into my coming-of-age sixteenth birthday.

From that day on I received a new perfume every Christmas, each in a distinctive bottle and with its own story: the oriental Shalimar; the woody, balsamic, now lost, Sortilège; Ma Griffe by Carven; and a bold chypre, Femme by Rochas. These perfumery rites of passage culminated in my mother's gift of Chanel No. 5 for my twenty-first birthday. The simple iconic flacon inside the white box trimmed with black and the modern aldehydic top note signaled I was officially a grown up. I bought my first little black dress, one of many to follow, and a pair of sexy sling backs with four-inch heels.

How you choose to wear fragrance and in what form is entirely up to you. My daughter has worn the same perfume since high school. I like to change it up, mixing old with new and all the emotions in between. I wear Guerlain's L'Heure Bleu and the modern scents of Jo Malone. I immerse myself in the fragrance stories behind the compositions of Carlos Huber, Serge Lutens, and Miuccia Prada, and I'm like a child at Christmas, in anticipation of Superstitious, a fragrance collaboration between Alber Elbaz, the former Creative Director of Lanvin, and French perfumer Frédéric Malle.

I have friends who forego perfume but wear aromatherapy oils, others who cannot go a day without a vase of flowers on their desk or the chance to clip herbs for a family dinner. The olfactory landscape is vast and layered with possibility.

Of all our senses smell is most closely associated with memory. That's why a whiff of Aramis might remind you of a college boyfriend, a spritz of lavender becomes your grandmother's lace handkerchief, and a field of peonies takes you back to the joyful spring days of your childhood.

Dab a perfume or a natural oil on your wrist, and whenever your hand passes in front of you, so will the scent and you'll smile. Press citrus aromatherapy oils on your temples for renewed energy. Dab lavender on your pillowcase for a soothing night's sleep.

Bring fragrance, flowers, and herbs into your world, no matter how frenzied your life. Take the time to smell that tomato, the basil leaf, the violets, and your freshly laundered sheets. As the most powerful of our senses, smell takes us from ordinary to extraordinary with the speed of a bullet train. It goes right to the brain and navigates its way to the heart.

TWENTY-EIGHT

COMPETITION AMONGST WOMEN IS OVERRATED

"Well behaved women rarely make history."
Eleanor Roosevelt

We like to celebrate and build up other women. One evening in Trastevere in Rome, I was having an aperitivo with my husband. At the table next to us, two Italian women in their fifties talked about their summer holidays in Procida. I couldn't help interjecting as I've dreamed about going to that rainbow island for years. My husband offered them a second aperitivo, and they invited us to share a small box of chocolates. Dusk was settling in over the Tiber, and I was just so happy to be where I was.

At that point, a young woman arrived on a *motorino* with her boyfriend. She was stunning, dressed in form-fitting leather from top to bottom, striding across the sidewalk in skyscraper stiletto boots I would break my neck in. She had thick curly auburn hair and wide green eyes that reminded me of Marisa Berenson in *Cabaret.* As she kissed the café owner on both cheeks and settled in a table, the two women next to us commented on what a beauty she was. They talked about her shapely torso, her perfect legs and her magnificent eyes. *Like the turquoise waters of Sardegna*, said one woman. It was as if they were marveling at the sculpture of Pauline Bonaparte in the Borghese Galleries.

Finally, one of the women shouted across, "*Sei Bellissimma*." The young woman blushed and toasted them. We all toasted. She and the boyfriend joined us, and we ordered antipasti to share. Life was good. The sky turned a glorious rose. The aperitivo was delicious, and we were in the company of women saluting each other. The ensuing conversation was about the joys of youth and chance encounters.

If you ask me, competition is colossally overrated. There are only two types that have merit: the competition with oneself to do better, and the competition within sports or commerce whereby you face off against a competing team, athlete, or company. That's it. Competition within the team or organization is at best a distraction.

The concept of women always in competition with one another is both cynical and outdated. Years ago, when I ran the training department for the U.S. affiliate of a large cosmetics company, I was introduced to my cohort in the Canadian office. For whatever reason, some people in the company tried to stoke a competition between us. Our first encounter disappointed anyone hoping for a catfight. We became good friends. We worked together, playing off each other's strengths, offsetting each other's weaknesses, and accomplishing some awesome work.

I'm reminded of the story about Marilyn Monroe and Ella Fitzgerald in the 1950s. The owner of the Mocambo nightclub refused to let Fitzgerald sing there. So Marilyn made a phone call. She promised him that if he let Ella sing, she would take a first-row table every night. Given Marilyn's movie star allure, the owner complied. The rest is history. Once the public heard Ella sing, there was no stopping her. In return, she convinced Marilyn to take voice lessons to strengthen her own strong singing voice. It's sad that this story about Marilyn never garnered the same media attention as the photos of her emerging from JFK's birthday cake.

But years later, the noted feminist and journalist Gloria Steinem wrote a touching biography of Marilyn. She told us the story of a smart, compassionate, and complex woman we never got to know. Instead, we were given an exaggerated image of what women were supposed to be, childlike and ornamental. Perhaps if we'd have a movement then, as Steinem explains, we could have saved her life. She would have known she was not alone, and she was not what she never wanted to be — a "joke." That a leader of the feminist movement could connect so deeply with the innermost feelings and fears of America's most iconic sex symbol speaks to our inherent and profound connections as women. Our greatest strength is our willingness to comprehend instead of judge.

It's propitious that I was finishing up this book during the 2016 Rio Olympics. Watching young athletes go after their dream reminds us that the world's future is brighter than we believe. But the image that stands out the most is that of American runner Abbey D'Agostino placing her hand on the shoulder of Nikki Hamblin, the New Zealand runner she'd accidentally clipped from behind. Abbey didn't know she'd injured her ankle. She was too focused on helping Nikki up. She urged her not to quit.

The two women had never met before, but they came together in that precise moment to show the world what the Olympics are all about. They both finished the race, even with Abbey's injury, and the Olympic committee declared both runners would be in the finals.

In a recent New York Times editorial, Facebook's Sheryl Sandberg challenged the queen bee stereotype head on. If it ever existed to the degree we believed, it has diminished as more women rise to positions of power in organizations, start their own businesses, or make other life-affirming decisions. Whether it thrives or not is irrelevant. Once women make the conscious choice to celebrate and support other women, make the conscious effort to break with conventions about how they should "behave," they just do it. And the result is nothing short of extraordinary.

For Italian women, we know it's the thread of human connection that favors collaboration over competition. Life practices are tethered to family and community. To underscore this unshakable commitment, I feel compelled to reference the opening scene in *The Godfather*, as much as it pains me. As an Italian-American, I rile against the persistent stereotypes of Italians as Mafiosi. But Coppola has done something brilliant here. He has violated all the rules of screenwriting to craft a thirty-minute opening scene. It is set in Don Corleone's office on the day of his daughter's wedding. We see a dignified Marlon Brando, as Vito Corleone, interact with family, community members, politicians, businessmen, and gangsters.

One of his strongest criticisms of a local businessman is that he never once invited him for a coffee. In thirty minutes, twenty-seven minutes longer than most opening scenes, we feel and understand the palpable interlocking threads in all those relationships. We know what this family holds most dear, and what Michael Corleone, who will emerge as film's protagonist, holds in his hand.

Avid filmgoers will remember the most talked-about scenes of violence and revenge through all four *Godfather* films, and comment on Michael's reflective silence at the end of the final episode, but what they miss is the film's central theme: Power destroys Family. By showing us the united Corleone family in the long segments of that first scene, we understand more deeply what Michael relinquishes. At the end, after consistently choosing power over community, he's lost everything and everyone he's ever loved. His family.

Consider the Oscar acceptance speeches made by Italian actors, directors, and composers. Antonioni accepted his honorary Oscar with almost childlike humility. Fellini diverted attention from himself to give credit to those who worked with him and to thank his wife, Giulietta Masina.

Most recently, the brilliant composer Ennio Morricone finally received his first Oscar for best original score. He accepted it with deference to Quentin Tarantino, Harvey Weinstein, and his fellow nominees, declaring that "there isn't a great soundtrack without a great movie that inspires it." Years earlier, when presented with an honorary Oscar for creating over five hundred musical scores for film and television, and more than one hundred classical works, he merely commented that this was not an ending but a point of departure for all he still had to learn.

While Sophia Loren waited, in Rome, to hear if she'd been awarded the Oscar for best actress, she didn't work on an acceptance speech. She made pasta and she called her mother. It seems appropriate that when the news finally came, a dear friend and member of her inner circle delivered it. When she was awarded an honorary Oscar by Gregory Peck thirty years later, she confessed to her fellow actors that on that first night in Rome, she had been too scared to face anyone. But that tonight she was not alone. Her husband and her two sons were in the audience, as was the film community she now felt so much a part of.

Acknowledge an Italian's accomplishment, and he or she will direct that acknowledgement to others. She understands that we are connected to a large, significant community of others on a profoundly visceral level and that the nurturing parts of our nature must be harnessed to further those connections.

In her book *Old World Daughter. New World Mother*, Maria Laurino describes this as "that thorny personal and public dilemma — to reconcile the quest for individual freedom with the need for collective responsibility." For the Italian-American woman, it becomes a question of balancing an American culture of self-sufficiency and individualism with the Italian and European ethos of building a collaborative, interdependent, and sustainable community. Those two forces are in constant battle with one another as they go back to the question of identity. We stand inside and in between two cultures, weighing the merits of each against the daily challenges of modern living.

Within this evolving framework, there is much Italian women bring to the world. I'm reminded of a New York Times editorial "The

Italian Military to the Rescue," written by Beppe Severgnini. The title is meant to provoke humor, but Severgnini confronts the stereotype head on. He explains that "Italy's military history can boast more heroes than good armies." The problem is not about courage, but about a country that does not like war. Italians, by character, are more inclined to construct bridges than tear them down, to embrace those in need versus turning them away, to build communities instead of burning villages, and in general to build rather than destroy.

As examples, he cites Mare Nostrum in the Strait of Sicily, where the Italian Navy and Coast Guard rescued over 139,000 migrants arriving from Libya, Syria, and Eritrea, and the generosity of local civilians there provided refuge, nourishment, and medical care to those not drowned at sea. In another instance, in a Kosovo NATO-controlled camp, Italians arrived to find great unrest between the Serbs and Roma families and the Albanian Kosovars. Instead of taking sides, the Italians organized a soccer tournament. Tensions that had been building for months lifted away. In both these instances, community is the central conceit around which better solutions are formed. What Severgnini describes is a feminine approach to conflict, an Italian approach rooted in humanity, one that seeks to understand, build, and transform. It underscores the imminent value of bringing more female voices to the negotiating table and into public office. And raises the bar on the potential to achieve extraordinary outcomes.

TWENTY-NINE

SECRETS OF AN ITALIAN WOMAN'S SKIN

"It is a cuisine both uncomplicated and refined and whose clean, balanced tastes depend on fresh ingredients, simply but knowingly prepared."
Lorenza de Medici, author and chef

I t's inevitable. You return from Italy, you catch a glimpse of yourself, and something's changed. You receive compliments on how beautiful you look. Your skin, subtly bronzed and with a hint of pink on the cheeks, is as luminous as silk. You exude a glow that can only come from one place. Inside you.

It comes from eating authentic and delicious food flushed with moisture and nutrients — from vegetables and fruits left to ripen under the sun on tree branches, rich in vitamins and the minerals of volcanic soil, and harvested at their peak. In the U.S., produce is picked before it is ripe, thereby losing the infusion of nutrients from an already depleted soil. This is why tomatoes in Italy are so sweet and succulent you can pick them off the vine and eat them like fruit, and why when you return to New York and bite into one of those mealy pinkish orbs from the supermarket, you want to cry.

But the problem goes deeper. It's buried inside our depleted soil. Today, fruits and vegetables grown on over-farmed U.S. land yield a fraction of the nutritional benefits they did fifty years ago. Traditional small farming methods, in contrast, evaluate the bottom line via a community-based model comprised of three vital factors: social, environmental, and financial. Modern fast-farming methods consider only the monetary, fostering the breeding of evermore varieties of high-yield, pesticide, and climate-resistant crops. As the crops grow bigger and more rapidly, nutrient uptake slows and depletes the soil.

To put this in perspective, today you have to eat five apples to get the natural vitamins, minerals and nutrients in a single apple eaten in the 1950s. Try to remember, if you were lucky to have experienced it, what an apple tasted like back then. You can have some of that experience if you go to a small apple orchard or visit a heritage farm in Vermont or New York. Each bite, depending on the variety, has its own balance of tartness and sweetness. If you close your eyes, you can distinguish a Honey Crisp from a Cortland, a Macintosh from a Roma, and a Fiji from a Macoun. Its varietal yields such flavor, you wouldn't consider substituting a sugary or processed dessert for the pleasure of eating fresh fruit. Taste the farm's homemade apple cider without sweeteners or additives, and you will never drink the commercial versions again. Real food needs no embellishment. Italians have always known that.

My journeys in Italy are infused with joyful food memories, full of distinctive and genuine flavors with provenance. They evoke the colors and smells of their birthplace: the cold white peaches in Santa Margherita in Liguria; the fresh tomato on the perfect pizza in the port of Naples; the Prosciutto di Parma alongside sweet melon in a trattoria under the arcades of Bologna; the sunny yellow lemons squeezed over grilled calamari in Amalfi. One afternoon my daughter and I ordered up a plate of melon and prosciutto, along with a Caprese salad of tomato and bufala mozzarella in an off-the-beaten-track bar off the Via Venti Settembre in Rome. It was to have been our antipasto, but it was so good we ordered it twice.

Go to the simplest trattoria or bar anywhere in Italy, even in one of the poorest neighborhoods. Avoid tourist spots and you will find simple, fresh, organic food. Unlike the U.S., this is the rule and not the exception. A good espresso, a plate of pasta, fresh greens, fresh fruits, and hormone- and antibiotic-free meats and dairy are not luxuries or an elite concept. They are fundamental to good health and to the creation of a sustainable community. There is no such thing as organic in Italy. All food here is organic. And sadly, so was it once in the United States. Yes, there was a time when all our food was organic and we could ascribe to the dictum of Michael Pollan: "Don't eat anything your great-grandmother wouldn't recognize as food."

An Italian family who goes to a ski resort will most likely pack their own lunch. But if they don't, they can sit at a table on a terrace below the craggy slopes of the magnificent Dolomites and order up a plate of pasta, a salad, and a glass of wine. They can do the same at the beach where they might opt for *frutti di mare*. At a soccer game or a rest stop along the autostrada, a *porchetta* sandwich may be in order. This is yet another way to sustain family tradition, community, good health, and a daily quality of life envied around the world. It is not surprising that when Italians emigrate, they take their culinary practices with them.

Most Italian dishes everywhere along the peninsula use fresh ingredients, including local olive oils, and have a high water content. This is a perpetual spa for your skin, the body's largest organ, which needs a steady daily infusion of Omega 3s, moisture, and plant nutrients to thrive and look its very best.

Here is more good news. Good, fresh food satisfies, so you eat less of it.

Consider these two examples.

You buy a commercial chocolate bar. You think you will just eat a small piece, but you eat all of it and wonder why you would do such a thing.

Alternatively you choose a dark chocolate truffle by Jacques Torres. Because the first taste is so yummy, you pause. You finish on the next bite, but you do so slowly, because you want the pleasure to take full effect. You may or may not have a second one. You will not eat a third. You're satisfied and have in effect, consumed fewer calories than with the larger, processed chocolate.

Drink a single espresso corto prepared by a Roman barista, and you will not order a second.

Or, pour a huge cup of watery commercial coffee at an auto stop in a strip mall, and you will keep re-filling your cup without ever feeling satisfied.

Food scientists employed by industrial and fast food companies manipulate foods so the public will eat more of them. They know and exploit the chemical basis for this. Processed foods and fast foods are specifically formulated to stop just short of the satisfaction point, so the body craves more. The minimal nutritional value in these foods also contributes to these cravings, as do select ingredients engineered to make certain snack foods, like chips, addictive. They induce people to eat more, even though they may not even like what they're eating.

To an Italian this is an outrage. When you are raised to eat well and *sano*, as my mother says, processed food has no appeal or reason for being. In the same spirit, an Italian woman will never eat a sugar-free, fat-free, or anything-free piece of chocolate. She will have good real chocolate, and simply eat less of it.

"Eat food. Not too much. Mostly plants," says Michael Pollan in *In Defense of Food*. It should be required reading. In its pages, I find the echo of my grandmother and my great-grandmother, of Ada Boni's Talismano, and of generations of Italian women who knew that the extraordinary is woven into the fabric of a country's soil and sun. It is embedded in good, clean, and fair food practices that foster the health and wellness of generations to come. We didn't need a movement back then. It was simply the way we lived.

And this is why, when you are in Italy, I want you to tear up the guilt like an old movie ticket and live all'italiana. Savor your cornetto, spremuta, and cappuccino every morning. Take long walks everywhere. Get lost.

When you meet friends for lunch or a *spuntino* in the middle of the day, by all means have a plate of the local specialty, perhaps a pasta or a salad or a caprese, whatever appeals, with a glass of wine, some water, a piece of bread. Leave the trattoria and have an espresso at the bar.

Mid-afternoon, if you are in Rome, when you stand in front of La Fontana di Trevi, there is a delicious little gelateria to your right. I don't know the name, but it's been there forever. It's been written about in travel magazines, and everyone who goes there loves it.

Have a gelato — one or two flavors with a dollop of panna, which is true fresh cream, not the aerosol kind. Indeed, whenever you see a true gelateria or cioccolateria artigianale go inside. If the gelato is truly artigianale and preservative-free it will be stored under steel lids. The names of the flavors will be printed alongside. The gelato will not be artificially colored. Your first clue: pistachio is not bright green. It's pale and almost gray. And absolutely experiment. For instance, there are fascinating differences between Sicilian and Tuscan gelato — so discover them. I'm not sure what they are, but I plan to keep tasting until I do.

Before dinner, stop for an aperitivo, perhaps an Aperol Spritz, a Campari, or a simple sparkling Prosecco, perfect as the light changes and the air cools. The waiter may bring you chips and nuts, or a few morsels of creamy parmigiano. The chips will be elegantly arranged in a small bowl so you take one at a time. Peanuts are served with a tiny spoon so you drop them into the palm of your hand and taste each nut in-between sips of your drink and conversations with friends, or as you sit alone in a piazzetta in Pescara after a swim and a day on the beach.

This is how I grew up.

THIRTY

COLLABORATIVE LOVE

"Their smiles and laughter are due to their habit of thinking pleasurably aloud about the pleasures of life. They have humanity rather than humor, and the real significance of the distinction is seldom understood."
Luigi Barzini, writer

We know about the Italian woman's commitment to family. What's equally significant is her innate ability to seek out and cultivate community in ways uniquely Italian.

Many years ago, while choosing a middle school for our daughter, my husband and I visited La Scuola d'Italia Guglielmo Marconi. Known for its small class sizes and bilingual curriculum, La Scuola, where tuition is markedly lower than the norm, is a gem few people know about because this exceptional little school does so little to market itself.

As Steve and I made the prerequisite rounds of other private and public schools, we were subjected to elaborate presentations about technological superiority, grade point averages, and college admissions stats. We left each session loaded down with catalogues and business cards. To manage the sheer volume of data, we set up a spreadsheet outlining the advantages, disadvantages, and costs of each school. Our heads were spinning, and we were no closer to a decision. Something that should have been simple had become ridiculously complicated.

Enter a hand-written invitation to La Scuola D'Italia for a personal meeting with the headmistress and the teachers of the school. It was scheduled in the evening to accommodate working parents and to not disrupt the school day. On the evening of the event, we entered a stately Edwardian building on East 96th street. The Italian flag hung outside. La Scuola students dressed in navy and white greeted us in a marble foyer and led us up a winding iron staircase to the third floor. Along the way, we passed the children's artwork: paintings, pastels, poetry, and essays written in cursive, each signed proudly by the student.

As we approached a splendid marble arch outside the reception room, we heard the music of Rossini. A pianist in the vestibule by the window nodded as we entered. Inside the room were banquet tables set with flowers and flutes of Prosecco. An attendant in a white waistcoat carried trays of canapés. I was immediately hungry, especially after I saw him pass with an assortment of bruschette — tomato, artichoke, and cannellini bean.

Just as I was about to grab one, the headmistress, dressed in a superbly elegant cocktail dress, introduced herself. She asked for our names, and repeated them to make sure she'd pronounced them correctly. She asked smart, thoughtful questions about our child and why we were interested in La Scuola. She listened so well and with such impeccable eye contact, I'm sure she could have repeated our responses word for word.

Most appealing was that La Scuola was trilingual and multicultural. From Pre-K through the *liceo* (high school), classes were taught in both Italian and English. In sixth grade, French was added as a third language. Its curriculum, rooted in the European classical tradition, emphasized a strong foundation in liberal arts, mathematics, and science, and our daughter would interact daily with children from other parts of the world.

What we didn't say, but realized afterwards, was how at home we felt from the moment we'd entered the entrance vestibule of the school. Perhaps it had started earlier, with the hand-written invitation that implied we were already part of the community. I compare this with the experience of the other schools, where one felt very much like an outsider trying to earn entry into an exclusive club.

After that evening we knew on a gut level that this was the school for us. Italians are masters of simplicity and clarity. What they are not good at is self-promotion. For many years La Scuola D'Italia remained one of Manhattan's best-kept secrets. Some grades in the *liceo* were so small they had only nine students. But in spite of the inevitable challenges, the school remained true to its mission and word spread, not only to interested parents but also to the Italian business and financial community. I'm happy to read that they have opened an expansive modern facility, steps from Lincoln Center, the plans of which include an adult learning center to advance Italian culture and language.

I recently spoke with another Italian-American writer about the Italian aversion to self-promotion. We don't like to introduce ourselves or talk about what we do for a living. Self-promotion is considered bragging. By contrast, to laud another is an act of communal generosity. Ask us to write a testimonial or make a speech praising the work of a colleague, and we dive in. Ask us to write an elevator speech about our business, a bio for the back of our book cover, or a profile on LinkedIn, and we freeze.

Where does this come from? There are several possibilities. A belief that one's work should speak for itself, thereby rendering acknowledgment unnecessary. That would feed directly into Guadagno's description of working *italianamente*: You give it your all and the result is evident. Maybe it's something else — the supposition that self-promotion gives preference to the individual over the community, thereby upending the Italian penchant for collaboration and generosity. Then there is the third possibility, the pervasive Italian belief that our social contract in all matters of achievement, consumption, and production respect the trifecta of global responsibility: environmental, humanitarian, and monetary. Given the international scope of this mission, the fruits of the contract can only be achieved through community and collaboration.

A shining example is Carlo Petrini's Slow Food Movement. It started in a moment of passionate dissent. McDonald's was about to open in Piazza di Spagna. Petrini, a journalist, and a group of fellow activists staged a protest by serving up plates of penne. Their motto: We don't want fast food. We want slow food.

In 1989, Petrini and his acolytes founded the International Slow Food Movement to promote the study of food culture and environmental sustainability. They signed the Slow Food Manifesto advocating good, clean, fair food. Good food is seasonal, local, fresh and delicious. Clean food preserves biodiversity. Fair food respects fair labor practices and cultural diversity.

Today, Slow Food is active in 160 countries and has over 150,000 members. In 2013, Petrini addressed the UN Permanent Forum on Indigenous Issues, and he spoke at the "Global Food Security and Nutrition Dialogue" at the UN Conference on Sustainable Development. That same year, the Slow Food International Congress in Torino greeted 650 delegates from 95 countries, and ratified a policy document, *The Central Role of Food*. Every two years, Slow Food hosts the Salone del Gusto, the world's largest food and wine fair, in collaboration with their annual Terra Madre world meeting of food communities, drawing together over 250,000 visitors.

How did a plate of pasta protest by a handful of people in the late '80s give rise to an organization that effectively challenged the dominance of Big Food, fast food, and industrial giants like Monsanto?

They started with the convivia, local chapters that gather people together around growing, cooking, and sharing food. It is, once again, about the community — smaller regional communities first, then national communities, and finally the global community. Slow Food has a decentralized structure. The leader of each chapter brings a team together to promote local farmers, local artisans, and local flavors through farmers' markets, planting school gardens, social gatherings, tastings, and regional events.

In this way, Slow Food — and Italy more broadly — fills the emptiness that comes with enriching ourselves via the wrong things with a belief system that honors humanity and environment. It forces us to slow down and recognize the things in life that bring enduring joy. Take note of that feeling when you are in Italy. It's that sense of fulfillment that powers the passion to create and to live fully. And in whatever way you can, bring it home with you. You will make your own life and the lives of those around you extraordinary in ways you had never imagined.

THIRTY-ONE

TEARS

"If you haven't cried, your eyes can't be beautiful."
Sophia Loren

On the first day at La Scuola d'Italia, my daughter burst into tears. As I tried to comfort her, I braced myself for one of two reactions from the office staff. They and surrounding parents would look at us with annoyance, or they would call in the school psychologist to assess my daughter's separation anxiety. Neither happened. The staff members shrugged and went about their work. People cry. It's a natural human reaction to a myriad of human emotions, whether fear, love, joy, stress, or confusion. And sometimes it's catharsis. Let her have a good cry, and when she's ready, she can go into her classroom.

In Maria Laurino's intelligent and touching book *Old World Daughter, New World Mother*, she describes how she unexpectedly burst into tears during her son's graduation. I've been there. I'm familiar with the sudden flood of tears that comes with no provocation. I'm at my daughter's graduation and I'm fine, but when she walks onto the stage to retrieve her diploma, I start sobbing — as I have at her first communion, her first birthday, at every Mother's Day card she's ever written to me in her beautiful script on hand-drawn cards, and at every graduation I've ever been to, including my adult nephew's graduation from medical school.

Laurino writes how her eyes would fill at witnessing the opening scenes of the film *Cinema Paradiso*, the mother calling her son so many miles away, the announcement that his dear friend and mentor had died, and the scenes of his old town in Sicily. And what all this brings to mind to me, even after all these years, is nonna Laura washing clothes in the fountain. It brings back that evening at home when my father had to tell my mother that nonna Laura was very sick and that she had to fly that night, back to Antrosano, to see her for the last time.

In the closing scene of *Cinema Paradiso*, Salvatore hooks up the old film reel as his dear friend Alfredo did years ago when Salvatore was a child nicknamed Toto, and he sits alone in the old theater watching all the films of his childhood. He cries. And I do too. On Mother's Day, a Facebook friend sent me a YouTube video of Pavarotti singing "Mama" and well...I don't have to tell you. Play any one of the old Roman ballads, especially "Vecchia Roma" or "Roma non fà la stupida stasera" sung by Nilla Pizzi... and I lose it. My daughter will shake her head and say, "I know, Mom — you're way too sentimental about this stuff."

At Christmas time or after returning from Italy in their later years, when my parents would go on their own, my mother always brought me a special gift. It might be a knit jacket from a *magliaia* in Avezzano, a tiny purse from a leather artisan in Chieti, or a pair of shoes. For my brother, there would be silk ties and leather belts. She had and still has an eye for picking out the most unique item in a shop. Every time she handed out her gifts and saw our beaming faces, she would cry. The joy of giving us something that made us happy was too much for her. I have a photo of my father on Christmas Eve. He's holding up his camera to take a picture of my mother, and his eyes are all red because he has just surprised her with her first and only fur coat. My father had the warmest, kindest eyes.

We played opera on most evenings in summer, on the gramophone back then. Out rang "Un bel dì" from *Madame Butterfly*, "Che gelida manina" from *La Bohème*, "Brindiamo" from *Traviata*, or the jubilant processional from *Aida* — and we would all be gushing tears, my father more than anyone. In deference to Plotkin, opera is one of Italy's most respected artistic treasures. On a human level, it's also good for the soul.

When Sophia Loren presented the Oscar to her good friend Gregory Peck in 1963 for his performance in *To Kill A Mockingbird*, she gave him a tearful embrace. Almost thirty years later, in 1991, he presented her with an honorary Oscar. We will never forget her heart-stopping descent down the stairs in a sparkling black-sequined dress and her eyes, made all the more beautiful by her tears, sweeping the room to embrace her fellow artists. Even before she spoke to her community, she'd delivered her message.

Crying for the Italian is a natural expression. It is in some ways a treat. It feels good. So please, have a good cry, whenever or wherever you feel the need to, and let others see you. There is a collective sensibility around certain public displays of emotion. It reconnects us as fellow human beings. It makes us slow down. Not to mention the big fringe benefit: You will feel a whole lot better afterwards. And what I've just shared with you is the Italian alternative to psychotherapy.

THIRTY-TWO

TIMELESS RAIMENT OR SUSTAINABLE CHIC

"Businesses depend on demand. It is time now to develop a conscious and large demand for decentralized, humanely farmed fiber systems."
Rebecca Burgess, founder of Fibershed

As Spagnoli, Ferretti, and Cucinelli continue to design, sew, and produce with dogged adherence to heritage and sustainability, a cadre of visionary and socially conscious entrepreneurs in other parts of the world are transforming the clothing landscape in ways we never would have imagined.

In a sky-lit white studio space won the Emeryville/Oakland border in California, a young knitwear designer named Emily Cunetto works on two knitting machines not unlike the one my mother worked on over seventy years ago. As you enter her studio you see cones of naturally colored cotton and swatches of locally sourced wool fibers pinned along the walls. Among her projects is a series of knit swatches for a Wool and Fine Fiber book created in collaboration with Rebecca Burgess of Fibershed.

This project for Cunetto was a dream come true. As a former photography student drawn to textiles, she took to creating swatches of knitwear patterns for a variety of yarn shops. Eventually Cunetto connected with Rebecca and with other local suppliers and artisans, all of whom shared her vision — that of crafting beautiful knitwear from organic and sustainable local sources. The timing was right as the world is starting to listen, but it's always been.

Working on the swatches made Cunetto all the more aware of the different textural qualities inherent in the fibers within her bioregion. One of the most beautiful designs in her collection is a stylish grass-feed top, a contemporary swing jacket with a retro feel. She wanted to design something she herself would like to wear, suited to the cool Northern California temperatures. This too had its genesis in a collaboration with Jacalyn Post of Sheep to Shop, who created the custom yarn from a mixture of fibers, including alpaca and guanaco, the latter known for its warmth and unusual softness. Post sourced all the yarns from other environmentally conscious suppliers, thereby enhancing the natural connections that drew these artisans together, an integrated human ecosystem emanating from a love of fiber and fabric and from the immutable relationship between source and final product. Every step of every process respects provenance.

Rebecca Burgess' Fibershed Project began in 2010 when she set out to reduce her own ecological footprint by developing a wardrobe whose dyes, fibers, and labors were exclusively sourced from the region surrounding her corporate headquarters, an area no larger than 150 miles. She reached out to build partnerships with farmers and local artisans within the community. They would draw upon the natural dyes, regionally grown fibers, and local talent to create clothing made by hand. She'd never expected her initiative would spawn a global movement and a cooperative green business model designed to establish and grow sustainable textile producing communities. Her Grow Your Jeans initiative, which launched in 2015, takes from the soil and the community, creates objects of beauty, and gives back to the land and its people.

The Grow Your Jeans process is exactly what it claims. It starts with the planting and harvesting of the indigo plant for a natural dye that does not use metallic mordants to achieve the color. Afterwards, the dried leaves are stomped by human feet, composted, and later fermented in water, homemade hardwood wood ash lye, and crushed lime. It takes nine to ten months from the planting to the dyeing process, which is applied to 100% non-GMO cotton to make the jeans. The cotton crop is planted and harvested each year. The cotton is then shipped south for seed removal, and then to North Carolina mills where the fiber is combed and spun into yarn, which will be woven into the denim fabric in a studio and artisan workshop in San Francisco. Here Leslie Terzian Markoff works on a human-powered Macomber floor loom. She uses no fossil fuel, derived slashing agents, or the resins required by electrical looms. I think here about that famous Fritz Lang quote: *"The heart is the mediator between the head and the hand."* When you work this way, you can't help but invest your heart in it. And a product created with heart is far more beautiful and enduring than one created without it.

Sally Fox's métier began with a spinning hobby and a handful of renegade seeds. She discovered that the lint of certain cotton seeds contained brown not white color and began to imagine cotton in natural colors that would not require environmentally harmful dyes. She discovered, however, that while the color was attractive, the fiber wasn't as long or as resilient as white cotton, something difficult to change via crossbreeding. Undeterred, Fox suggested a process of cross-pollinating the brown and green lint cottonseeds with the white cotton plants. Her idea got a cold reception from other growers, so she moved out to California with a family loan, bought a breeding ground, and set up her own production. She called her company Foxfibre. That was in 1989. Today, Foxfibre cotton is sold to major textile and clothing manufacturers including Fieldcrest, LL Bean, and Lands' End.

"It takes time to make something truly beautiful. I make wholesome clothes that embody connection with all that surrounds us, the universe."

In her small atelier in New York's West Village, Jussara Lee, a Brazilian designer of Korean descent, creates custom-made designs using sustainably sourced materials. In the way she lives and works, she echoes the Italian consumer ethic of my grandmother: Compra meno, compra meglio. Buy less, buy better. Lee's timeless, original designs are created around a love of simplicity and understated sophistication. The looks are fresh and contemporary, without catering to commercial or superficial trends. Lee believes that while slow fashion is, for the moment, expensive, it will become more affordable as demand rises. When we consider the true costs behind the over production and disposal of cheap clothing, including time spent shopping, the feeling that one never has anything to wear despite overstuffed closets, and the unfair wages paid to garment workers around the world, it's the current cost that's staggering and unsustainable.

Fortunately that is changing. Consumers, especially millennials, are placing a renewed emphasis on quality versus quantity and on more ethical business practices with respect to the food they eat and the clothing they wear. In a recent article in *The Atlantic*, "*The Power of Buying Less by Buying Better,*" the authors cite a survey by a British charity that discovered most women's garments are worn only seven times before disappearing to the back of a closet or discarded. A series of documentaries and books targeting the wastefulness in mainstream fashion, *The Shockingly High Price of Cheap Fashion* by Elizabeth Cline, and the shocking documentary, *The True Cost*, all illustrate in stark numbers the environmental and labor costs of trendy, cheap, easily disposable fashion.

Along a similar vein, a minimalist lifestyle and the 'less is more' ethic is taking root. I hear nonna Laura in heaven clapping her hands. If she were alive today, she would send me a copy of Marie Kondo's *The Life Changing Magic of Tidying Up*. It's everything she taught me. Have less, do more. The difference between style and fashion is quality. The latter, she borrowed from Giorgio Armani, who understood fit better than any other designer.

She would applaud current developments in the online fashion retailing community. Initiatives like those of Emily Cunetto, Fibershed, and Jussara Lee are building. Recently, a twenty-five-year-old British designer launched the 30-year Sweatshirt, a pullover finished with a treatment that wards off shrinking and pilling. The company promises repairs free of charge until 2046. Its shirt, like the shirts and the clothing I've seen on my Italian friends, never look worn. Walk along an Italian street, even in the smallest village, and you will notice that people's clothing looks fresh and new.

Another San Francisco-based retailer, Cuyana, sells elegant and feminine wardrobe staples crafted from premium fabrics and leathers created through ethical relationships with their suppliers and inside their factories. Zady and Everlane sell quality basics at affordable prices. Since these are online retailers, they save on brick and mortar expenses, wholesaling and retailing markups, thereby better able to control pricing. The trend toward better quality clothing that one respects, loves wearing, and holds onto is on track and gaining momentum.

In the meantime, in the West Village, Jussara Lee walks the talk. Her shirts are made in a small facility close to her atelier. She interacts face to face with her suppliers, and like Burgess, Fox, and Cuneo, believes that the people behind the scenes are the true magicians in the production cycle. Their smiles validate a collaborative process that's working. In her designs, Lee uses only sustainably produced raw materials. Nothing is wasted. She even uses mismatched mother of pearl buttons. Believing that excess creates a sluggish life, she asserts that all a woman needs in her wardrobe are three pairs of pants, five shirts, two hand-tailored jackets, three dresses and two skirts. She lives in a small apartment, runs a small atelier, and bikes to work. Luxury is based in this freedom.

The stories of Emily, Jassara, Rebecca, and Sally are resonant of the work of Spagnoli, Cucinelli, and Ferretti in the fashion world, as well as that of the devoted followers of Carlo Petrini's Slow Food Movement. Both Slow Food and Slow Fashion tackle the high speed, impersonal, and centralized systems that deliver cheap food and clothing at an escalating cost to humanity and our environment. We lose what matters most: heritage, connectedness, and quality of life. Artisans and farmers in Italy and in other parts of the world have always known this.

It was nonna Laura who taught me the extraordinariness to be found in slow creation. So many years ago now, I held my hands out as she unfurled each strand of ivory angora wool and rolled it into a tight ball. Beside her was another ball of coarser wool in a rainbow of Missoni-like colors. "The colors of fields and sunsets," she said. I wonder how, as I child, I managed to sit still for so long until she was satisfied and the ball was plump and smooth, flawless in its shape and unity. I knew where my mother's *mani d'oro* had come from.

Six months after that evening a package arrived from across the ocean. Inside, wrapped in lavender tissue, was a knitted bolero in the colors of fields, sunsets, and white clouds. Nonna Laura had woven in pink toggle buttons and loops so it would close warm and cuddly against my neck. The colors and the design were so unusual, my friends wanted to know where I'd bought it. I told them its story. They listened, awed. It's in my possession to this day.

EPILOGUE

One of my fondest memories is of an eighth-grade school trip to the United Nations. Most vividly I remember our guide pointing out a huge tapestry. She said it had been woven from a single thread that could wrap around the equator four times. Along the way it was dyed different colors. It was so long ago I don't remember the design, but the idea of a thread wrapping around the center of the world over and over again remains imprinted in my mind.

Perhaps, in some respects, it represents the human experience and the collaborations we form as we create our lives. We shape our own communities and mini communities. Along the way, we redefine what community means.

Relinquishing the melting pot and mosaic theories of integration, I prefer that of the tapestry.

A tapestry's thread is pliable and dynamic. As it weaves, it encounters obstacles. It changes course, its pattern evolves, it discovers its story along the way and reinvents the journey. Even as each culture's story weaves its own ethos, our inter-connectedness as a world is inevitable.

When I see Gisele strut across the Olympic platform in seven-inch heels and in glowing celebration of her Brazilian heritage, or Serena Williams hold up her racket in victory as she opens a school in Kenya, or Claudia Cardinale bring together her North African ancestry, Italian nationality and French upbringing to advocate for the rights of girls and women of the Mediterranean, or Lady Gaga take up a crusade against bullying and domestic violence, I know the tapestry is on track.

The tapestry thread is infinite. The tapestry itself is portable. It can be moved from one location to the next. Today it may hang in the United Nations. Tomorrow it may be in a museum. As one sews, one makes mistakes because the path to the dream is uncertain. So what does one do? One works with the imperfection. It is the texture of life.

In her book *In Other Words*, Jhumpa Lahiri writes about the feeling of imperfection as she learns to speak and write in another language. She favors the state because it gives dimension to the journey. What is perfection anyway? Who defines it? We are on the precipice of learning that perfect and normal are subjective terms and that by subscribing to them, we blindfold ourselves to the richness around us.

What is inevitable is that the tapestry thread will keep going. It will expand its reach and bring all cultures into its purview. Its path is one of inclusion. The world will become richly more diverse. History will not be stopped.

So while this book is about Italian women, it is in many ways reflective of all women and all cultural groups in every corner of the globe. It's that same thread, dyed in different colors and weaving the life patterns of the future. It circles the world over and over again, the ordinary fiber of life transformed into the extraordinary art of living.

AUTHOR BIOGRAPHY

Gabriella Contestabile is the author of the novel, *The Artisan's Star,* and owner of Su Misura (Made to Measure) Journeys; a boutique travel concept for the female traveler who relishes off-the-beaten-track adventures that celebrate the Italian way of life.

This book/travel initiative has its roots in her pre-writer life as a foreign language teacher, later as Executive Director and Vice President of International Training in a number of global companies (including Estee Lauder, Shiseido, and Prada Beauty) where she would create immersive and unconventional learning experiences in unique settings around the world.

One of her favorite pastimes, wherever she is in the world, is to scout out the best, and most 'Italian' espresso in the hood. It requires multiple tastings, but that's the idea.

Gabriella was born in Italy, and raised in Ottawa and New York City, where she currently lives with her husband, her mother, and a furry Shih Tzu named Oreo.

SASS, SMARTS, STILETTOS, AND THE SU MISURA (MADE-TO-MEASURE) LIFE

Ah, that inimitable Italian style. It's embedded in an Italian woman's DNA. Fashion doesn't define her. She defines herself. She knows that an extraordinary life is not about status, money, or achievement. The only mastery it requires is one her heritage has given her, the irrepressible passion to make art of life itself.

She doesn't follow trends and she doesn't follow rules. She embraces tradition and rejects convention. For her life is a gift. Everything is a reason for wonder. The hard stuff is just a provocation to shake things up.

Ask an Italian woman where she gets her sense of style and she will tell you it's not about labels. It's tethered to humble roots; humanity, community, conscious consumerism, and a profound appreciation for art in all its forms.

Sass, Smarts and Stilettos takes the reader on a journey from the humble hill towns of Abruzzo to the revered fashion capitals of Milan and Rome, into the artisan workshops of Florence, and the humanistic business practices of Luisa Spagnoli, Brunello Cuccinelli, and Alberta Ferretti, from the emergence of Italy's fashion industry after WWII, to slow food and sustainable fashion initiatives taking root around the world.

Life lessons echo in the words of the author's mother and grandmother, in the voices of Italian film divas, designers, tastemakers, writers, and artisans across generations, from the first Sala Bianca in Florence to the game changing design ethic of Franca Sozzani, Miuccia Prada, and Donatella Versace.

Learn how to live fully within your own philosophy of living. Say good-bye to mindless consumerism, emotional clutter, and others' expectations. Create a personal style that fits like a custom blazer by Ferrè and enchants like the colors of a Sicilian sunset. Then go on to craft an extraordinary and empowering life made-to-measure for you alone.

Sass, Smarts, and Stilettos has given you the template.

Now join us on our next journey. Experience 'the Italian way' first hand through our Extraordinary Women Travel Initiative, a moveable sensory feast through Tuscany in 2018.

From the mountains of Carrara where Michelangelo sourced his marble, to the quirky fashion finds in the markets of Forte de Marmi.

A fascinating escapade to learn about the sumptuous fabrics of the Antico Setificio Fiorentino, exquisite Chianti wineries, and the art of hospitality from Florence's most innovative hoteliers.

To contact or to interact with Gabriella, or to learn more about Su Misura journeys….

www.gabriellacontestabile.com
www.sumisurasensoryjourneys.com
www.facebook.com/SuMisuraSensoryJourneys
www.instagram.com/sumisurajourneys
www.linkedin.com/in/gabriella-contestabile

Gabriella's Memberships and Affiliations

ALLi - Alliance of Independent Authors
Authors of Influence Community
NYC Leadership Council: BIAAG – Because I Am A Girl-Plan International
Casa Italiana Zerillo-Marimò, New York University
National Organization of Italian-American Woman
New York Italian Women

Six Figures for Accomplished Women
Slow Food USA
Women Speakers Association

Writings and Publications

"The Artisan's Star", a novel
"Experiencing Italy Italianamente" – travel e-book

Acknowledgments

It takes a community of extraordinary people to turn a writer's vision into a book.

Thank you to....

My publisher, Julie Salisbury, for believing in me and in this book. For inspiring me through insight and example to go deep, tell the bigger story, and 'get it written'.

The Inspire-a-Book and Authors of Influence communities who gave me a focus, a template, and the drive to keep writing.

A brilliant and visionary team of artisans; masters of their métiers, whose talent and dedication made art of my words.

Editors: Catherine Michele Adams and Fernanda Pinzon.

Illustrator and graphic artist: Katerina Miras.

Portrait Photographer: Catherine Michele Adams.

Typesetter and Project Manager: Greg Salisbury.

In alphabetical order: Christine Czark Atkins, Jose and Maria Barrera, Francesca Belluomini, Flavia Brunetti, Angela Carpio, Bert Contestabile, Ornella Fado, Alessandra Gardin, Aleksandra Lacka, Karen LaRosa, Marie-Elena Liotta, Guy, Anna, Roberta and Rose Lynn Marino, Linda Sorgiovanni, Laura Stegmann, and Maria Zoccoli.

Family on both sides of the ocean, especially those who are no longer here, but whose stories echo inside these pages: Francesco e Laura, Umberto, Angelina, Cecco, Peppino, Minicuccio, Antonella, Lauretta, Franco, Dominic, and Thea.

Finally, my deepest gratitude to...

My talented and insightful daughter Daniela, who taught me there is more than one way to be a feminist.

And always Steve, whose support and razor-sharp wit made every day of this project, like every day of our lives together, extraordinary and funny as hell.

BIBLIOGRAPHY

Books

Bolton, Andrew, Harold Koda, & Judith Thurman, Schiaparelli and Prada, Impossible Conversations, Metropolitan Museum of Art (New York, 2012).

Bolton, Andrew, Manus x Machina: Fashion in an age of Technology, Metropolitan Museum of Art (New York, 2016).

Boni, Ada, The Talisman: Italian Cook Book, Crown Publishers (New York, 1950).

Czerwinski, Michael, Fifty Dresses That Changed the World, The Design Museum (London, 2009).

Fava, Claudio G. & Aldo Vignano, The Films of Federico Fellini, Citadel Press, (New Jersey, 1984)

Gill, Anton, Il Gigante, Michelangelo, Florence, and the David:1492-1504, MacMillian (New York, 2002).

Lahiri, Jhumpa, In Other Words, Alfred A. Knopf (Toronto, 2015).

Laurino, Maria, Old World Daughter, New World Mother: An Education in Love and Freedom, W.W. Norton & Company (New York, 2009).

Loren, Sophia, Yesterday, Today, and Tomorrow, My Life, Simon & Schuster (New York, 2014).

Stanfill, Sonnet, ed., The Glamour of Italian Fashion Since 1945, V&A Publishing (London, 2014)

Articles

Buckley, Re'ka, "Glamour and the Italian Film Stars of the 1950s," Historical Journal of Film, Radio and Television, Vol 28, No.3 (August 2008).

Charleston, Beth Duncuff, based on original work by Harold Koda, "Christian Dior 1905-1957," The Costume Institute at the Metropolitan Museum of Art (New York).

Cline, Elizabeth, "The Power of Buying Less by Buying Better," The Atlantic (Feb 16, 2016).

Cruz, Elyssa da, "Made in Italy: Italian Fashion from 1950-Now," The Costume Institute at the Metropolitan Museum of Art (New York).

Daniels, Jess, "Making Clothing with a Local Pedigree," Fibershed (Resilience) (January 2016).

"FIRENZE: Made In Italy, The Dream of the Sala Bianca. How Giovanni Battista Giorgini Invented Italian Fashion in Postwar Florence" (May 2013)

Hazan, Marcella, "An Introduction to Italian Cuisine," made-in-italy.com.

Mead, Rebecca, "The Prince of Solomeo, The Cashmere Utopia of Brunello Cucinelli," The New Yorker (March 29, 2010).

Petkanas, Christopher, "Creating an Italian Cashmere Kingdom in Umbria," Travel and Leisure.

Plotkin, Fred, "Performing Opera Italianamente," WQXR: Operavore (July 20, 2015).

Scientific American, "Dirt Poor: Have Fruits and Vegetables Become Less Nutritious?" (April 27, 2011).

Severgnini, Beppe, "The Italian Military to the Rescue!" International New York Times (Oct. 17, 2014).

Slow Food USA, "From Field to Frock: The Promise of Slow Fashion," (Spring 2016).

Seminars

"The Godfather: A Special Screenwriting Seminar in 7 Act Structure," by Jacob Krueger

Slow Fashion: FIT Seminar, "From Field to Frock," Fall, 2016

Italian Glossary

Dear reader,

There is nothing quite like the sensation of speaking the Italian language, whether it is native to you, or acquired. You change. You do indeed, start to speak with your hands, but also with your eyes, your voice, and ultimately, your heart.

I've used numerous Italian words throughout the book within a context to make them understandable in English. Just for fun, I've listed some translations here.

"A Napoli si mangia bene"
A phrase that means 'one eats well in Naples'.

Aperitivo
A pre-dinner drink; generally a Campari, Negroni, Aperol. Their colors always make me think of a sunset.

Aperol Spritz
A popular summer aperitivo. Aperol is a mild, low alcohol bitter, served with Prosecco for a refreshing spritz.

Artigiano
Artisan.

Atelier
French word for a workshop or studio usually owned by an artisan/ designer.

Autostrada
Highway.

Bacio (gelato)
Rich chocolate, blended with chunks of real hazelnuts.

Bistecca alla Fiorentina
A grilled T-bone steak usually from the Chianina or Maremma breed of cattle.

caffè (lower case)
Italian word for coffee, which always means espresso. You don't ask for an espresso at the bar. You ask for a 'caffè'.

Caffè (upper case)
Designates a place as in Caffè Greco, Caffè Florian, Caffè Canova.

Calamaretti
The tiniest calamari. Hard to find, and delicious.

Calzature
Any type of shoe.

Cinecittà
A large film studio in Rome, built during the fascist era and dubbed 'Hollywood on the Tiber'.

Cognoscenti
Those who are "in the know".

Contadina/Contadino
A farmworker.

Cornetto
A crescent-shaped pastry similar to a croissant and sometimes filled with marmalade or cream. A morning favorite consumed at the bar with a cappuccino.

Da morire ('to die for')
Not found in this text. But now that you know how to compliment the handsome cameriere who brings you an aperitivo and a smooth wooden board of tasty stuzzichini (small plates), go ahead and book your flight to Rome. You are as ready as you'll ever be.

FIAT cinquecento
Small FIAT popular in the 1950s.

Frutti di mare
Seafood.

Gelato
Italian ice cream, made with milk, cream, sugar, and natural flavorings. Generally lower in fat than other varieties.

Gianduia (gelato)
Another chocolate and hazelnut mix, but smoother and with milk chocolate. The original gianduia by Perugina was the precursor to Nutella.

Granita al Caffè
Shaved espresso ice often topped with panna (fresh whipped cream).

Grappolo
Grape cluster.

Guarda!
Look!

Il bar
Where Italians go for a morning espresso, non-alcoholic drinks or evening aperitivi. The 'bar' is to Italy what the 'café' is to France, the 'taverna' is to Greece, and the 'pub' to Ireland.

Il Talismano della Felicità
Literally means 'The Talisman of Happiness'; apropos name of the first Italian cookbook ever written, by Ada Boni.

La Bella Figura
A good first impression. Also refers to presenting oneself in the most gracious and elegant way in any setting.

Limoncello
A lemon liqueur traditionally made from the zest of the Femminello St. Teresa lemons, also known as Sorrento lemons.

Lungotevere
The road that runs along the length of the Tiber in Rome, connecting Piazza del Porto di Ripetta to Ponte Regina Margherita in Campo Marzio.

Magliaia
Someone who makes garments by intertwining yarn or thread. An artisan of knitwear.

Marsala
A sweet wine from Marsala in Sicily.

Mozzarella di Bufala
A mozzarella made from the milk of the Mediterranea Italiana buffalo. A specialty of the Campania region.

Nocciola (gelato)
Hazelnut.

Oeuvre
French word designating a 'work', usually a work of art.

Ospedale
Hospital.

Ospedale Pediatrico del Bambin Gesù
The Pediatric Hospital of Baby Jesus.

Motorino
Motorbike.

Nonna or Nonno
Grandmother/Grandfather.

Panna
Fresh whipped cream spread on top of gelato and eaten with a tiny spoon.

Passeggiata
A leisurely stroll in the afternoon or the evenings, usually in stylish dress, preferably on the way to one's local bar or gelateria.

Pecorino
Cheese made from ewe's milk.

Pistachio (gelato)
True to its name and made from the best pistachios, usually from Sicily.

Porchetta
Moist, fatty, boneless pork roast.

Quadrattini
Tiny, square wafer cookies with multiple thin layers and filled with hazelnut, chocolate or vanilla cream.

Quattrocento from millequatrocento
The years 1400 – 1499, collectively referred to as il quattrocento; years of significant cultural and artistic achievement in Italy.

Ribollita
A hearty Tuscan bread, vegetable, and cannellini bean soup.

Sarto/Sarta
Tailor/Dressmaker.

Scopa
Literally means 'broom' in Italian. It's also the name of a card game where the winner swoops up all the cards.

Sfoglia
The thin sheet of pasta dough first rolled out as thin as possible before we cut it into shapes for tagliatelle, lasagna, and ravioli.

Smoking
Nothing to do with cigarettes. This is the Italian and French term for tuxedo.

Spaghetti Cacio e Pepe
A Roman specialty - spaghetti anointed with just black pepper and pecorino cheese. The word 'cacio' is in dialect.

Spremuta d'arancio
Fresh squeezed orange juice, ideally from Sicilian blood oranges.

Stracciatella (gelato)
Light vanilla with slivers or chunks of dark chocolate.

Vietato Sporgersi
Leaning out the train window is prohibited. But Italians don't follow rules.

CPSIA information can be obtained
at www.ICGtesting.com
Printed in the USA
FSOW01n2357071117
40747FS